THE ISLAND OF STABILITY

and other stories

Omid Iranikhah

STORIES

THE ISLAND OF STABILITY

"The dreams of men, the seed of commonwealths, the germs of empires."
-Joseph Conrad, *Heart of Darkness*

1

Once again, I see nothing.

Once again, the questions.

"Are you a Tudehi?"

"No."

"Are you a Marxist?"

"No."

"Are you a Mujahid?"

"No."

He lights a cigarette and blows the smoke in my face. I hear the saliva swim around in his mouth as it forms into a grin.

"I can't imagine a slut like you being an Islamist. But, what's the harm in still asking? Are you an Islamist?"

"No."

"Then again, I hear all about how those bearded hypocrites love the company of a good whore as much as the next man. Perhaps you fell under the spell of one of them. Perhaps he brainwashed you with lies and slander against His Majesty."

"I'm a married woman."

"I am well-aware, Mrs. Hashemi," he responds promptly. "What would your husband Bijan think if he found out his wife was being passed around by mullahs? What would your son Kian and your daughter Mersedeh think? What would the public think when we release it to the press? Would you ever be able to sell another painting?"

"I don't know any mullahs. I'm not Muslim."

"Are you a Tudehi?"

"No."

"Are you a Marxist?"

"No."

"Are you a Mujahid?"

"No."

"Are you affiliated with any group or persons who would dare speak out against His Majesty, the King of Kings?"

"You'd have to throw just about every single Iranian in jail if that's your criteria."

"But every disease must begin somewhere, Mrs. Hashemi. You had to have learned these lies somewhere. Just give me a name. One name, and this will all be over."

"I've told you everything I know."

"Did you learn it from your husband? I wouldn't put it past an intellectual like him to fall prey to communist propaganda."

"No."

"Then where did you learn to speak and write such filth about His Majesty? What gave you the audacity?"

"I'm not affiliated with any organization. They're my beliefs and mine alone. I've given out a public apology. I've signed whatever you told me to sign. But I *do not* have any names to give you. Please, for the love of God, believe me."

He laughs and takes another drag of his cigarette. Footsteps. I feel his breath on my neck.

"You must value whoever it is you're protecting a lot more than your husband and children, Mrs. Hashemi."

"I'm not protecting anyone!"

"He must satisfy you more than your husband does, hm?"

"Please let me go. I don't know anything."

"Of course you don't know anything. An artist should know better than to bite the hand that feeds them. The arts have always meant a great deal to His Majesty. Do you think a mullah gives a damn about art? A communist? Art is worthless to these traitorous demagogues you've chosen to align yourself with. All you are to them is just another fine piece of cunt they can have their way with. Is that what you want your legacy to be, Mrs. Hashemi?"

"No."

"Then I will ask you again, are you a Tudehi?"

"No."

"Are you a Marxist?"

"*No.*"

"Are you a Mujahid whore?"

"No!"

"Are you affiliated with any group or persons who would dare speak out against His Majesty, the King of Kings?!"

"No! Go to Hell!"

"Go to Hell, huh? Keep talking to me like that."

Once again, I hear him unbuckle his belt.

***

December 31, 1977
Niavaran Complex, Tehran
*A Toast from President Jimmy Carter to His
Majesty, the Shah of Iran (abridged)*

*"Your Majesties and distinguished leaders
of Iran from all walks of life: I would
like to say just a few words tonight in
appreciation for your hospitality and the
delightful evening that we've already
experienced with you. Some have asked why
we came to Iran so close behind the
delightful visit that we received from the
Shah and Empress Farah just a month or so
ago. After they left our country, I asked
my wife, 'With whom would you like to spend
New Year's Eve?' And she said, 'Above all
others, I think, with the Shah and Empress
Farah.' So we arranged the trip accordingly
and came to be with you.*

*These visits and the close cooperation that
we share, the intense personal and group
negotiations and consultations are very*

beneficial to both our countries. They are particularly beneficial to me as a new leader of the United States. I might pause parenthetically and say I apologize for taking 10 years off your service this afternoon when I said 27 years. It should have been 37 years. And Empress Farah, thank you very much for correcting me on that. The Shah said he felt 10 years younger when I did that.

But we do have a close friendship that's very meaningful to all the people in our country. I think it is a good harbinger of things to come—that we could close out this year and begin a new year with those in whom we have such great confidence and with whom we share such great responsibilities for the present and for the future.

As we drove in from the airport this afternoon to the beautiful white palace where we will spend the night, and saw the monument in the distance, I asked the Shah what was the purpose of the beautiful monument. And he told me that it was built several years ago, erected to commemorate the 2500th anniversary of this great nation. This was a sobering thought to me. We have been very proud in our Nation to celebrate our 200th birthday, a couple of years ago. But it illustrates the deep and penetrating consciousness that comes from an ancient heritage and a culture that preceded any that we've ever known in our own lives.

Recently, Empress Farah gave us a beautiful book called 'The Bridge of Turquoise'—and we get many gifts of that kind from visitors—and for a few days I have to admit that we didn't pay enough attention to it. And one night I started to thumb through the pages, and I called my wife, Rosalynn, and I called my daughter, Amy, who climbed into my lap, and we spent several hours studying very carefully the beautiful history that this book portrays of Persia, of Iran, of its people, of its lands, of its heritage and its history, and also of its future. It caused me to be reminded again of the value of ancient friendships and the importance of close ties that bind us as we face difficult problems.

Iran, because of the great leadership of the Shah, is an island of stability in one of the more troubled areas of the world."

2

FROM: *Dr. Miranda Bailey <mbailey@sjhs.com>*
TO: *Cyrus Ghorbani <cghorbani@ucla.edu>*
DATE: *February 15, 2023, 12:04 PM*
SUBJECT: *Bullying Incident at School*

Dear Mr. Ghorbani,

I would like to let you know that earlier this morning, it came to my attention that last Thursday during lunch, a student by the name of Sam Afshari called Parham a derogatory slur. We have a zero tolerance policy on hate speech, so once Parham confirmed to me that Sam called him the slur, I took necessary disciplinary action on Sam. I offer my sincerest apologies to both you and Shireen that such a vile word was directed at a student of this school. I can assure you that it will never happen again.

Best Regards,
Dr. Bailey

***

FROM: *Cyrus Ghorbani <cghorbani@ucla.edu>*
TO: *Dr. Miranda Bailey <mbailey@sjhs.com>*
DATE: *February 15, 2023, 12:31 PM*
SUBJECT: *Re: Bullying Incident at School*

Hi Dr. Bailey,

Thank you for letting me know. We'll talk to Parham about this when he gets home today. One question though: What do you mean by "derogatory" slur?

Best,
Cyrus Ghorbani, Ph. D. (he/him/his)
Professor of Iranian Studies, UCLA

***

FROM: *Dr. Miranda Bailey <mbailey@sjhs.com>*
TO: *Cyrus Ghorbani <cghorbani@ucla.edu>*
DATE: *February 15, 2023, 12:35 PM*
SUBJECT: *Re: Bullying Incident at School*

The slur (which I will not repeat) was directed at Parham's ethnicity. It was specifically a slur used to demean people of Middle Eastern descent.

Best Regards,
Dr. Bailey

***

FROM: *Lisa Afshari <lisadraws79@afshari.com>*
TO: *Dr. Miranda Bailey <mbailey@sjhs.com>*
CC: *Maziar Afshari <maziar@afshari.com>*
DATE: *February 16, 2023, 1:02 AM*
SUBJECT: *Regarding Sam*

Hey Miranda,

My husband and I have spoken to Sam to get to the bottom of what happened at school last Thursday. Bigotry of any kind is absolutely unacceptable in our family, so as you can imagine, it came as a total shock when you told us about what he said to this boy. He is profoundly sorry and accepts full responsibility for his actions. After talking it over, Mazi and I decided that it would be healing for both parties if we could get together with Parham's parents sometime this week to get to know each other <u>as people</u>. We're not familiar with the family, so would you please give us their contact info so that we can reach out to them?

Thanks,
Lisa <3

3

Shireen had just had her nails done.

It had been two weeks since she'd last had her nails done. That was two weeks since the previous time she'd had her nails done, and so on. It was tradition. Every other Wednesday. Most of the time, it was a basic manicure and pedicure. A cleaning, followed by the filing and buffing of the cuticles and a massage of her hands and feet, and then a re-painting. She favored more neutral colors. Ivory, beige, cream, and so on. She never thought she would enjoy it so much, let alone look forward to it.

It began as a way to stop chewing her nails. For a while, it was working. She wouldn't chew her nails as a young girl. As a young girl, she couldn't. Regular inspections at school in Iran meant her nails needed to be cut neatly. Short, but not too short. No visible dirt under them either. A moist reed to the hands stung like hell. She'd gotten it once over a small fungus under her left pinky nail that looked enough like a cloud of dirt.

It began with picking her hair. She would pick her hair whenever exams would come around, and then in the weeks leading up to her first wedding. She was fourteen. On the day of, her mother did her best to cover the bald spots with a hairstyle that was fashionable at the time.

"You wouldn't want to ruin something so beautiful, would you?"

Beauty was always the most reliable cutoff point of all her bad habits. Once it got in the way of her beauty, the sensation ceased to be satisfying. Her phase of pulling out her thick eyelashes, for example, was short-lived because it started to be noticeable within a few days. She could get away with pulling out the hairs on her head for much longer. By a certain point in her life, she'd had it down to a science. She knew exactly which spots on her head to pull from so that it would be a little over a month before she'd need to temporarily quit cold turkey. As she waited for her hair to grow back, she'd chew her nails. For a while, she left her bad habits behind with that life.

Now a thirty-year-old woman living in a new country with a new husband, Shireen began chewing her nails again. She didn't notice her left hand move up to her mouth. She didn't notice the taste and texture of the newly dried cream-colored nail polish until she'd already bitten off a corner of the nail on her thumb. She didn't notice it until the bitterness invaded her tongue, and then she spit it out.

It happened after a call from Cyrus. He gave her the rundown. Some kid at school called Parham a racial slur. Her

Parham. Parham the quiet math whiz who had stopped speaking to her in his native language in order to lose his funny accent. Parham who would always tell her everything. Last Thursday? This happened last Thursday and he never told her anything? *He knows he can tell me everything, right? Have I not been there enough for him lately?*

Questions.

When she picked him up from school, he only confirmed what happened. She had more questions. He was done answering. Cyrus couldn't get a whole lot more out of him. The quiet boy was quieter than normal, and all they were left with were questions. *Sam Afshari? Isn't that an Iranian name? Is he Iranian? Why would an Iranian call him this? Why didn't you tell me sooner?*

Questions.

That was why they accepted the invitation. They did not want an apology, nor did they expect a sincere one. They wanted answers. Only then, they thought, they could move forward.

4

"*Riiight* there. Perfect. You guys are the best! And can we please, *possibly* move that coffee table so it can be between the two couches?"

Expensive paintings and sculptures from all over the world lined the walls and shelves of the spacious living room. Massive Persian rugs covered most of the freshly mopped marble floor, where the two maids of the Afshari family struggled to slide a heavy stone coffee table between a pair of sofas that had just been positioned to face each other. The pint-sized Salvadoran women were stronger than they looked, but even they had their limits. It was hard for Lisa to watch.

"Oh, you poor things. Okay, no more. Let's let the men of the house do some work for once, hm?"

Lisa headed for the stairs, "Mazi! Sam! Come help out!"

***

Beads of sweat dripped from the golden Faravahar pendant hanging off of Maziar's neck as he pedaled away on his Peloton. The balcony overlooked the fog-drenched green hills of the Pacific Palisades. Even with the view of the ocean on the horizon obstructed by fog, it was a sight worth its weight in gold. But Maziar's eyes were glued to the built-in screen on his exercise bike. A video of Canadian psychologist-turned-self-help-guru-turned-cult-personality Jordan Peterson interviewing Iranian activist and journalist Masih Alinejad, platforming the mass protests that had been going on in Iran since September to his millions of viewers. Was she aware of what this man stood for in the eyes of his loyal fanbase? A man whose pseudo-scientific justifications of so-called traditional gender roles and other mullah-esque talking points would hardly seem like the natural champion of a movement with women and queer people at its forefront. But to Alinejad, this man was invaluable. Finally, an influential figure in the West who was willing to tell the *truth* about the Trudeaus and the Obamas of the world and their cowardice in the face of the Islamic Republic. To Peterson, this woman was invaluable. Finally, a woman—a strong, outspoken *immigrant* woman—whom he could use as a weapon against Canada's Prime Minister.

Peterson smugly leaned back in his chair, repeatedly baiting Alinejad with pointed questions such as, *"So our Prime Minister is hypothetically a progressive-sort-of person and is hypothetically on the side of women and so how do you account for the fact that despite your attendance at the Canadian Parliament and your request for support that you never got it, how do you explain that?"* Maziar reveled in her sharp-tongued criticisms of the progressive Western leaders she dubbed *"regime apologists"* for opposing maximum pressure economic sanctions on the country from which she had been forced into exile.

Politics. Getting himself riled up about politics was the key to a great workout. No intense weight training session would be complete without the soothing, high-pitched wisdom of Ben Shapiro in his ears. He was sixty-eight and in the best shape he'd ever been. As a young man, he idolized Schwarzenegger and Stallone, but long workdays left him with little time to achieve his dream physique. Now semi-retired and wealthy beyond his wildest imagination, Maziar could dedicate himself to exercise.

"Mazi."

Lisa yanked an earbud out, "They're almost here, babe. Don't you wanna get ready?"

***

"Now, this is why I compare the Woke Epidemic to the early days of Hitler's rise to power. When you now have professionals who are bound by law to offer so-called gender affirming advice—bound by law—what do you call that? Have you ever heard of a therapist affirming a patient's identity? If you walk into a therapy session claiming you're the Messiah, they put you in the loony bin, and rightfully so!"

"Moron! Talk to one actual therapist! Bring one goddamn therapist onto your stupid show," Cyrus yelled into the stereo of his Honda Civic. He vented to his annoyed passenger, "I can't believe people buy into this guy's bullshit."

"If it makes you angry, then why do you listen to it?" Shireen asked in Farsi, as she would often do.

Cyrus, too, enjoyed getting himself riled up. As masochistic as it seemed, he felt from a young age that it was important to consume media from just about every camp of the political spectrum. "To be a good citizen is to be aware of these things," he would always tell his students.

"Just turn it off."

Cyrus obliged. He took a deep breath, tapping the steering wheel to fill the silence between them.

"Think we should stop at Trader Joe's or something?" Cyrus asked.

"Cherraah?"

"Might be a bad look if we show up empty-handed, no?"

"Then get something."

Cyrus nodded and thought about it.

"What should I get?"

"Cheh meedoonam? "

"A pastry? A pastry could be good."

Shireen shrugged, "Okay."

Cyrus thought about it some more.

"What kind of pastry?"

***

A rustic charcuterie board with jamón ibérico, bresaola, salami, and a collection of soft, semi-soft, and hard cheeses sat on the kitchen counter. Antonio was personally never a fan of cured meat, but the charcuterie board nevertheless became one of his favorite items to prepare for clients. It was a versatile hors d'oeuvre which could be endlessly customized to suit any occasion. If arranged with the utmost care and creativity, it had the power to transcend the very purpose of the hors d'oeuvre—a food meant to be passed around in social settings and consumed passively—and enter the realm of fine art. Of course, even the most visually appealing charcuterie board would fall apart without high-quality ingredients. If the client's budget allowed for it, Antonio sought only locally sourced ingredients such as—

"*Mmm*, I love this! You have outdone yourself, Antonio."

Lisa finished a lumpia—another one of Antonio's specialties—in two bites.

Maziar, now wearing a button-up shirt and jeans, entered the kitchen and headed straight for the stove to check on dinner. K*horesht karafs, khoresht gheymeh,* and *taaskabab*, along with a pot of basmati rice.

"Mazi, you have to try this lumpia."

Maziar licked his finger and swiped it along the side of the pot of rice. No sizzle yet. He turned to Antonio, "You're keeping an eye on this, yes?"

"Of course."

"Mazi, try the lumpia."

"When you see a sizzle here, it means the rice is crispy. See? It's not ready yet."

"I will keep that in mind."

"He's a professional chef. I think he knows how to make rice," Lisa laughed, making sure Antonio saw it.

*****

Holding a Snowflake Pastry from Trader Joe's in one hand and Shireen's hand in another, Cyrus marveled at the Spanish-style mansion before them.

"Damn."

Among the three cars parked on the driveway was a red Tesla Model S donning a bumper sticker of the words, *"WOMAN, LIFE, FREEDOM."*

* * *

Sam was too invested in his raid to notice his father coming into his room. Maziar pulled his headphones off.

"Dad, what the f—"

"You'll be in here the whole night?"

"Yes!"

"Okay. I'll bring you up some leftovers. No screaming at your game tonight, okay?"

"Okay," Sam huffed as he put his headphones back on. Maziar ruffled his son's greasy hair on his way out.

***

Cyrus rang the doorbell. He looked down at something, letting out an amused snort.

"That's funny."

He pointed at the doormat, which read, *"Hi, I'm Mat."*

"Get it?"

Shireen shook her head.

"Because it's a—"

The door swung open.

"Hiii! Welcome, welcome! It's so nice to finally meet you two!"

5

"What do you think? Should we go for it?"

"Go for it?"

"Their little olive branch here."

"There is no olives."

"No, see, when someone wants to like, offer something to apologize or make peace, we call that an olive branch. Then again, I *am* hungry."

Cyrus grabbed a small plate, helping himself to one of everything on the coffee table. "They have the upper hand for now, but don't worry, we'll get 'em back," he proclaimed as he stuffed his mouth with finger food.

Shireen chuckled, her eyes wandering to the artwork in the living room. Then, something seized all her attention.

"*Mmm*. Oh my God, this egg roll! Shireen, please try this."

Shireen approached a painting. A small painting that had an entire wall to itself, as if it were too special to be grouped with any other. A simple, old Persian-style painting of a harem of similarly dressed Qajar girls seemingly dancing around a fire.

"Found him," Lisa announced as she came downstairs with Maziar.

"*Salaam, salaam*. Welcome."

"*Salaam*."

"You are Koorosh?"

"Cyrus."

"Your parents didn't call you Koorosh?"

"Yeah, but everyone calls me Cyrus."

"Cyrus the Great! And you must be Shireen-*khanoom*."

"May I ask where you got this painting?" Shireen asked Maziar in Farsi.

Maziar walked over to the painting, "That, *azizam*, is a replica. It's the only replica we have here, actually."

"Is she asking about my painting?"

Shireen turned sharply to Lisa, "*Your* painting?"

"Well—"

Maziar cut in, "My family used to own the original in our home in Isfahan. It was my favorite painting, but we lost it when we came here, you know? I didn't know what it was called or who the artist was, so I could never find it. But, one day, one of my clients tells me about this website where you can describe any painting, and it uses AI technology to find it for you. And it found this one."

"So, I drew him a perfect replica and gave it to him for his birthday."

"You draw?" asked Cyrus.

"Oh, I can only copy other people's work. A useless talent."

"There is nothing useless about what you drew for me."

"Aww, thank you, baby."

"Let's sit. Come on," said Maziar as he led them to the sofas. The two couples sat across from each other.

"Hope you don't mind I helped myself to one of everything."

"Not at all, honey. That's what it's there for."

Maziar leaned toward Shireen, "You don't want anything, *azizam?*"

"*Na, merci, befarmaaeed.*"

"*Taarof nakon, beeyaah,*" Maziar forced a plate into Shireen's hand. "I can tell your husband is the American one."

Cyrus snatched another salami, "You guys just didn't seem like the *taarof*-y type."

"You're right. No *taarof* here. Stupid tradition. If I want something, I take it. If I don't, I say 'no' and that's it."

"*Eyval.*"

"What's a *taarof?*"

Maziar chuckled, "Just one of the many overly complicated rituals we Iranians love to put ourselves through."

"You were born here?" Lisa asked Cyrus.

"Yup. Born and raised in the Valley. Mom was barely pregnant with me when they came to America."

"That must've been hard for your parents."

"What year was this?"

"Nineteen eighty-four. What about you?"

"I was already here for college," Maziar answered. "And then, seventy-eight, my parents and my sister came."

"Wow. Good timing on their part."

"Well, they knew something bad was coming. My father, *khodaah beeyaamorzesh*, he worked for the government. If they stayed…"

Lisa sensed things were getting heavy. She shifted the focus, "Shireen, you didn't grow up here though, right?"

"No."

"How long have you been here?"

"Five years."

"Oh, wow, so you two met in Iran?"

"Oh, no. We…sorry, my English is not…"

"We met here. Shireen was, um…she was married once before."

"So, your boy…"

"He's my step-son," Cyrus clarified.

"It's good you got out. Good for you," Maziar said to Shireen.

"Yeah, Mazi tells me all the time how bad things are for women over there."

Shireen had no idea how to respond to that.

"But good things are happening now," Maziar commented proudly. "On the street, and now all the governments are taking notice. The world is finally seeing what *we* have been going through for the past forty-four years. *Inshallah*, those mullahs are on their way out."

"*Inshallah*," Shireen softly repeated.

"We have your generation to thank. Younger than you, even. Children. Brave."

"*So* brave," Lisa nodded along.

"And smart too."

"*So* smart."

Maziar kept going, "When the mullahs promise to reform this, reform that, you see through their lies. This will not be two thousand-nine all over again, I know that much."

Cyrus took another bite of his lumpia, "These egg rolls are magnificent."

"I know, *right?* They're called lumpia. I should've warned you, they're addictive."

"Are they homemade?"

"Our chef made them, actually. He's Filipino. I've gained like, fifteen pounds since we started hiring him."

"He have like, a recipe book, or…"

"That'd be bad for business if he just gave them out."

"But what if I steal it?"

Lisa laughed a bit too hard for such a mild joke.

"Really though, these are like, altering my brain chemistry. Have you had one yet, Shireen?"

Shireen took a lumpia and bit off the tip, "It's good. Thank you."

"You're welcome, honey. Enjoy."

The couples ate their lumpias. For about a minute, nothing could be heard but the sounds of crunches and the silence between each glance. Shireen to Cyrus. Cyrus to Shireen. Lisa to Maziar. Maziar to Lisa. Maziar to Shireen and Cyrus. Something needed to be said. No one wanted to be the first to say it.

Lisa cleared her throat, "Should we…wanna—"

Maziar set his plate down, "Yes. I think now that we… know each other a little bit…we should get into it now."

"Get it out of the way."

"True," Cyrus said with his mouth full.

"Don't wanna spend the whole night dancing around it."

"Yeah, no."

"Just gotta rip the Band-Aid off," Lisa made a ripping gesture, to no one's amusement.

Maziar gulped, "So…we like you."

"We like you too," Cyrus replied.

"Just from meeting you, we know…what's your boy's name, again? *Bebakhsheed.*"

"Parham," Shireen and Cyrus said at the same time.

"Parham. We have no doubt that Parham-*jaan* is a good boy, because clearly he comes from a good family."

"Wait, you thought he came from a bad family?"

Maziar and Lisa's faces went red, "No! Not at all!"

"No, I'm just…" Cyrus chuckled. Shireen shot him an icy glance.

Lisa leaned in, "We…invited you over because…well, first of all, it goes without saying that we are so *deeply* sorry—"

"Oh, it's not—"

"—and we want you to know that. That's the first thing. Words can have a lot of power. If there's anything we've learned in the past few years, it's that the whole 'sticks and stones' thing, that's not…words *do* have power."

"I agree."

"So…what my son said…" Lisa teared up. "Sorry."

Maziar rubbed her back, "Do you want some water?"

"No, I'm…hold on," she wiped her tears and composed herself. "What Sam called Parham at school was…inexcusable. It was unacceptable. It was reprehensible. It went against every value we raised him with. It went against everything I stand for, and especially everything his father stands for as an immigrant who— I'm sure—went through a lot of the same struggles your son is going through, and…well, both of you, really. What both of you went through. And…and still go through, I can imagine."

"Thank you. I appreciate—"

"And Sam is sorry too. He even…Mazi, do you have it?"

Maziar pulled a folded piece of paper out of his pocket and handed it to Cyrus.

"He wrote Parham an apology letter this morning. He likes writing by hand, since he was very little."

Cyrus began to unfold the paper.

"Um, actually, he'd prefer if only Parham reads it. Sorry."

"Oh, okay. Well, thank you," Cyrus stuffed the letter into his pocket. "We'll be sure to…give this to him."

Shireen opened her mouth to speak—

But Lisa wasn't finished, "I know it sounds like we forced him to write something—"

"No—"

"But we didn't. He's…he knows he has to grow and learn from this, as…as we all are. Growing and learning, I mean."

"Okay—"

"People like to say, '*Oh, everything's so politically correct now,*' and yeah, it can get overwhelming sometimes—especially for dinosaurs like us—but it's important to understand the hurt that our words can cause, y'know?"

Cyrus pursed his lips and nodded. *Is she gonna keep talking?*

"When I got the phone call from the school, I felt like someone just...punched me in the stomach. We were *both* shocked."

"You believe he said it though, right?"

"Oh, yeah, of course. He denied it at first, but…y'know, Mommy Lie Detector."

"And we knew we wanted to make things right. So, Lisa and I talked to him. Or, more like 'yelled' at first."

"We don't usually yell at him."

"He needed to understand how bad it was to say what he said."

"Absolutely."

"Then, he cried. She cried. I cried."

"We all cried together."

"And finally, he understood. You will read in that apology, he fully understands how much he hurt your *pessar*, and—"

Shireen finally cut him off, "*Bebakhsheed, vallee…*I appreciate your…apologizing, but…with all respect, I don't think it's enough because this was not the first time."

Maziar and Lisa leaned forward. Even Cyrus was taken by surprise.

"It's not?" Cyrus asked.

"No. Coming to this country with just me and him, it was not easy for him."

"I can imagine," Lisa said with a look of genuine sympathy that could easily be seen as patronizing.

"At the public school he went to, they were bad to him too. Making fun, calling names. And then, when I meet my husband, we…" Shireen ran out of English and looked to Cyrus for help.

"When we first started dating and I got to know Parham more, I could tell he was having a hard time. And he's a super smart kid. So, I told her, 'Look, I know we're barely past the honeymoon phase, but your kid deserves better. So, I'm not gonna ask for anything in return—like, even if we don't work out—but I think it's best that you put him in a private school, and I will handle the tuition.'"

Lisa put her hands over her heart, "That is so sweet."

Shireen sat up, "But as soon as he start going there, pandemic happen, so it was all computer for two years. Then, when he finally go back to school, the kids don't make fun of him but they ignore him. But he say one boy, Sam Afshari, was the worst."

"That is the first I'm hearing about this," Maziar remarked.

"How was Sam the worst?" asked Lisa.

"First, it start with making fun of his name. He call him, uh…Durham."

"Durham?"

"Why Durham?"

Cyrus shrugged, "I guess because 'Parham' kinda sounds like 'Durham.'"

Lisa shook her head, "Not really."

"A little bit. Parham, Durham."

"Is 'Durham' a curse word?" asked Maziar. "I've never heard of it before."

"It's a name."

"A name for what?"

"It's literally a name," said Cyrus. "Like *Bull Durham.*"

"What?"

"Y'know, the…baseball movie with Kevin Costner."

"So, he called him Kevin Costner?"

"No, I guess he'd just…never heard the name 'Parham' before and—"

"Or maybe he misheard it," Lisa suggested.

"Right, maybe Sam misheard it, and—"

Shireen cut Cyrus off, "He was making fun of him. Parham is not stupid. He know when someone is making fun."

"No one is suggesting that, *azizam.*"

"Okay, let's…" Cyrus put his hands up, trying to ease the tempo like a conductor. "So, Shireen, Parham would express to you that he felt hurt whenever Sam would call him 'Durham.'"

Shireen nodded.

"Okay, so that's what matters here."

"Right," Lisa agreed as Maziar did the subtlest of eye-rolls.

"And, look, kids would make fun of my name too, so I know how it feels. They'd call me 'Citrus.' Then, after *Con Air* came out, they started calling me 'Cyrus the Virus.'"

"But it start with making fun of his name, and then it get worse."

"So, you're saying Sam would bully Parham?" asked Maziar.

"Yes."

"What kinds of things would he do, exactly?"

"He…said rumors about him."

"What kinds of rumors?"

"I don't know."

"You don't know?"

"He won't tell me."

Lisa chimed in, "Well, you know how men are. Everything always kept inside—"

"But if he's going to accuse someone of that, shouldn't he be specific?"

"He did not accuse. This was just something he would, like…mention."

Maziar felt himself getting agitated, "Okay, what else would he do?"

"He…ignored him."

"But you say everyone in the school would ignore him."

"Yes, but this was different."

"How was it different?"

Shireen huffed, overwhelmed by the thoughts running through her head and having to translate them into a foreign tongue. She switched to Farsi, "When your child mentions something, you can tell—as his father—that something is bothering him, can you not?"

Maziar answered her in Farsi, "Yes, dear, but—"

"So, whenever he would mention Sam ignoring him, I could see it in his face that it hurt him more than when the other kids would. Now, why that is, he wouldn't tell me. But it did."

Maziar switched back to English, "Fair enough."

Lisa shrugged, "He says fair enough."

But Cyrus kept probing, "So, how long had this been going on before the, y'know…"

"From when they start going back to school."

"Why didn't you tell me any of this?"

"*Chon*…because I thought they would stop when they…get to know him."

Maziar tossed his hat back in the ring, "Here is what I'm wondering: When Sam called Parham…y'know…did Parham tell you about it that day?"

"No. We learned when you did."

"So, Parham didn't tell you what really happened when it happened?"

"Well, there were witnesses. That's how it got out to—"

"*Nonono*, I'm not saying that. I'm asking, what did you hear directly from Parham? I assume you asked him about it."

"He just confirmed what the school told us."

"And that's it?"

"What else he suppose to say?"

"Well, when we got that email, we questioned Sam for hours to get every detail."

"And what did Sam tell you?"

"He told us it started with Parham stepping on Sam's, eh… Michael Jordan shoes."

"But that's no excuse."

"I'm not saying it's an excuse, but it's important—"

"Why it's important?" Shireen asked.

"Because Sam is not a racist."

Lisa put a hand on Maziar's shoulder, "No one's saying that, honey. They know that. I mean, he's *half-Persian*, for Pete's sake!"

"Then why he call my son a nigger?"

All the air in the room was sucked out.

"Okay, he didn't say exactly that," said Cyrus.

Lisa nodded, "Right, he didn't. We should specify—"

"He said *sand*-nigger," Cyrus specified.

Lisa's face went red, "Can we…not use that word?"

"I think *I* can say it, as long as the 'sand' is in there."

"We can go without repeating it."

"Very well, but the fact is, it's a slur that's used to put down people like us."

"What if he didn't use it in a bad way?" Maziar suggested.

"Is there a good way?"

"No, but what if...okay, yes, it's a very bad word and no one should ever use it. But...you know how these kids talk to each other, so...maybe he used the word in a different way, like how the Black people do it."

Cyrus almost laughed, "Look, I teach at a university and I have never heard it be used in that way."

"Well, maybe not in front of you—"

"Have you ever been call that?" Shireen asked Maziar.

"Me? Of course! I was here back when those *ahmagh* kids in Iran took Americans hostage. Back then, they did much worse here than calling you bad words."

"Okay, but—"

"They almost burned down our house one night!"

"So, what, you're saying in the grand scheme of things, it's not a big deal that he said what he said?" asked Cyrus.

"No!"

"Mazi, regardless of the context, what Sam said to Parham was hurtful. I think we can all agree on that. There's no point in making excuses when—"

"I wasn't making excuses."

"Well, clearly, that's how they see it. Remember, we invited them over not to argue but to listen and learn."

"Thank you," said Cyrus. "And, look, I'm not...*we're* not here to be all accusatory and like, argue that what Sam said is in any way a reflection of how he was raised."

"It isn't."

"I know it isn't. I just...what confuses me is why. Like you said, he's half-Persian. Is he close with his dad's side of the family?"

"Yes. He grew up with his cousins."

"And that school is full of Persians, so I assume Sam has at least a couple Persian friends over there."

Lisa smiled innocently, "He has friends of all backgrounds."

"Okay, then. Have you ever heard him like, say anything disparaging about other races or ethnicities or anything like that?"

"Oh, no."

"Not even slurs, necessarily. Just like, maybe a stereotype, or…"

"Never. No. If anything, we're the ones he has to correct all the time with…y'know…which words aren't okay to use now, which words we should use, stuff like that."

"Kids know better than us nowadays," Maziar chuckled.

"So, then, how does someone like that call another kid a…"

Maziar sighed, "Why does it matter?"

"I think it matters because—"

"They're fifteen. Teenagers say things that are hurtful. It's not that deep."

"But I think we should really like, investigate these things because how else are we gonna move forward?"

Maziar persisted, "None of us can really know why Sam said what he said."

"Is he home right now?"

"Yes, he's in his room. Why?"

"Maybe we should ask him."

"I don't think that's a good idea," Lisa said through a nervous grin.

"If he wouldn't tell us, why would he tell you?"

"Does he spend a lot of time in his room?"

"Yeah…?"

"What does he do?"

"*Cheh meedoonam?* He plays online computer games."

"I was actually talking to Shireen about this the other day. You'd be surprised what these kids can get exposed to in those games."

"Mazi and I have always kept an eye on the kinds of games he plays."

"It's not the games; it's the people they meet on those games. One of my colleagues wrote a whole dissertation on extremist groups using games and social media to radicalize and recruit young men."

Lisa cupped her hands over her mouth, "Oh my God."

Maziar crossed his arms, "What does that have to do with anything?"

"Well, let's say Sam is playing a game with his friends, and then they end up in a lobby with a cool, charismatic guy who likes making vaguely racist jokes. Then, next thing they know, the guy turns out to be a neo-Nazi recruiter—"

"*Ooo, velemoon kon, baba!* You think neo-Nazis are smart enough to have recruiters who hang around online?"

"But these things happen."

"To these college people, anyone who makes vaguely racist jokes is a neo-Nazi."

"That's not true."

"What even is a Nazi nowadays? Everyone calls everyone they disagree with a Nazi."

"Well, see? There's a gray area there, and they know that."

"You're starting to sound exactly like my daughter."

"Your daughter?"

"Yes, my daughter. From my first marriage."

"She's a really sweet girl."

"Twenty-five. Very intelligent. Very hard-working. And then, I send her off to college. All of a sudden, *he's a Nazi. She's a Nazi.* Her own *father* is a Nazi! She doesn't even talk to me anymore because people like you brainwashed her with this woke nonsense!"

Before Cyrus could make his rebuttal, Lisa cut him off, "Okay, enough. That's not a word we can use lightly. My…I'm half-Jewish, and I had relatives who…"

Lisa's eyes once again welled up with tears. Maziar and Cyrus settled down.

"I just think that…as parents, it's our job to lead by example. Us pointing fingers at each other and creating more division…what kind of a message do you think we're putting out to the world? Now more than ever, it's important for us to come together and—even if we disagree on some things—find common ground."

Cyrus leaned toward Maziar, "I'm sorry for what I said, man. I can be a conspiracy nut sometimes, but I had no business dragging your kid into it."

"Thank you. I'm sorry too."

"See? That's something you guys have in common. Mazi also loves his little conspiracy theories."

Antonio stepped out of the kitchen and cleared his throat to get their attention.

"Sorry. Dinner is ready."

Lisa darted up, "Ah! Perfect timing. Nothing brings people together more than food."

Maziar motioned toward the dining room, *"Befarmaaeed."*

6

June 29, 1953
*A Message from President Dwight D. Eisenhower
to Mohammad Mossadegh, Prime Minister of Iran
(abridged)*

Dear Mr. Prime Minister,

I have received your letter of May 28 in which you described the present difficult situation in Iran and expressed the hope that the United States might be able to assist Iran in overcoming some of its difficulties. In writing my reply...I am motivated by the same spirit of friendly frankness as that which I find reflected in your letter.

The Government and people of the United States historically have cherished and still have deep feelings of friendliness for Iran and the Iranian people. They sincerely hope that Iran will be able to maintain its independence and that the Iranian people will be successful in realizing their national aspirations and in developing a contended and free nation which will contribute to world prosperity and peace.

It was primarily because of that hope that the United States Government during the last two years has made earnest efforts to assist in eliminating certain differences between Iran and the United Kingdom which have arisen as a result of the nationalization of the Iranian oil industry. It has been the belief of the United States that the reaching of an agreement in the matter of compensation would strengthen confidence throughout the world in the determination of Iran fully to adhere to the principles which render possible a harmonious community of free nations; that it would contribute to the strengthening of the international credit standing of Iran; and that it would lead to the solution of some of the financial and economic problems at present facing Iran.

The failure of Iran and of the United Kingdom to reach an agreement with regard to compensation has handicapped the Government of the United States in its efforts to help Iran. There is a strong feeling in the United States, even among American citizens most sympathetic to Iran and friendly to the Iranian people, that it would not be fair to the American taxpayers for the United States Government to extend any considerable amount of economic aid to Iran so long as Iran could have access to funds derived from the sale of its oil and oil products if a reasonable agreement were reached with regard to compensation whereby the large-scale marketing of Iranian oil would be resumed. Similarly, many American citizens would be deeply opposed to the purchase by the United States Government of Iranian oil in the absence of an oil settlement.

I fully understand that the Government of Iran must determine for itself which foreign and domestic policies are likely to be most advantageous to Iran and to the Iranian people. In what I have written, I am not trying to advise the Iranian Government on its best interests. I am merely trying to explain why, in the circumstances, the Government of the United States is not presently in a position to extend more aid to Iran or to purchase Iranian oil.

Please accept, Mr. Prime Minister, the renewed assurances of my highest consideration.

***

October 28, 1953
Eisenhower Diary (excerpt)

Another recent development that we helped bring about was the restoration of the Shah to power in Iran and the elimination of Mossadegh. The things we did were 'covert.' If knowledge of them became public, we would not only become embarrassed in that region, but our chances to do anything of like nature in the future would almost totally disappear.

Nevertheless our agent there, a member of the CIA [Kermit Roosevelt, Jr.], worked intelligently, courageously, and tirelessly. I listened to his detailed report, and it seemed more like a dime novel than an historical fact. When we realize that in the first hours of the attempted coup, all elements of surprise disappeared through betrayal, the Shah fled to Baghdad, and Mossadegh seemed more firmly entrenched than ever before, then we can understand exactly how courageous our agent was in staying right on the job and continuing to work until he reversed the entire situation.

Now if the British will be conciliatory and display some wisdom; if the Shah and his now premier, General Zahedi, will be only a little bit flexible, and the United States will stand by to help both financially and with wise counsel, we may really give a serious defeat to Russian intentions and plans in that area.

Of course, it will not be so easy for the Iranian economy to be restored, even if her refineries again begin to operate. This is due to the fact that during the long period of shut down of her oil fields, world buyers have gone to other sources of supply. These have been expanded to meet the need and now, literally, Iran really has no ready market for her vast oil production. However, this is a problem that we should help solve.

7

A giant painting of the sword-wielding Lion and Sun—emblem of the Persian Empire—loomed over them. They had all dug into their dinner by now, and glass after glass of wine loosened them up a bit. For a second, they had forgotten why they were there.

"Whenever I hear Mazi speak Farsi, it's like music to me."

"I tried to teach you."

"You taught me one curse word."

"Which one?" Cyrus asked.

"Beeshoor."

Cyrus laughed, "In all fairness, it's a versatile word."

"I'd like to learn more."

"Curse words?"

"No. Anything!"

"What me and him do at home is, I speak in Farsi and he speak back to me in English, so we learn each other's language," said Shireen.

"Yes, that's important," Maziar nodded. "With my daughter, we'd speak Farsi in the house because my first wife was also Iranian. But then, once she started school, all her friends were American, so, now she barely speaks it anymore."

"Mazi, I actually think after tonight, it would be a good idea to put Sam in a Farsi class. Y'know, to be closer to his roots."

"He doesn't know any Farsi?"

"He understands some words, but it's hard, especially because his mom—"

"Because you never taught me Farsi."

"Then how about I send you both to class?"

"Really?"

"Yeah, so you stop bothering me," he giggled

mischievously as Lisa hit his arm.

"So, you haven't been back to Iran since you left?" asked

Cyrus.

Maziar's smile faded, "Oh, no. I can't, because of who my

dad was."

"Your dad was pretty high up then, huh?"

"High enough."

"Have you been to Iran, Cyrus?"

"I spent a couple summers there as a kid and then I went

back in o-nine for a few months to cover the Green Movement."

"Cover, like journalism?" Maziar asked.

"Twitter."

"How do you think the protests now compare to then?"

"More organized, for sure."

"That's what I'm seeing too. You still have family there?"

"Few people, yeah. My grandma and a couple aunts and uncles, few cousins."

"You can still get in touch with them?"

"We do, but y'know, it's getting harder with the blockages."

"They have VPN though, right?"

"Yeah, but the government always finds a way to patch them."

"I programmed one myself. I can give it to you to pass along."

"Oh, thank you. That would be great."

"Of course. All my friends who have family there, they've been using it and it's still working, as far as I know."

"You make your own VPNs?"

"More of a hobby thing."

"Mazi's an inventor."

"Is that right?"

"I'm a programmer, not an inventor."

"But you like, invent programs."

"Was that always what you wanted to do?"

"Yes and no, um...I went to college for engineering, but...well, I come from a long line of great men...y'know, military generals, politicians, and then *I'm* going to spend my life sitting in an office? No. That was not my destiny. So, I dropped out in my last year."

"Wow."

"As you can imagine—you know Iranian parents—my parents weren't happy about it. They cut me off after that. Completely. Kicked out of the house, had to couch-surf. No contact for years."

"Jesus."

"It was very difficult. But it was the best time of my life, honest to God."

Lisa tipped herself onto Maziar, "The best time of your life?"

"Okay, second-best," he conceded and kissed her head. "But I am the man I am now because of that time, because it taught me the most important thing I've ever learned: personal responsibility. Now that I was on my own for the first time in my life, I learned the true value of responsibility for my own outcome."

"So, what'd you do?"

"Long story short, I started a small software company right when the internet was becoming a thing. Then, I ended up selling it and made some smart investments, so…"

"Well, good for *you*," Cyrus jokingly sneered. "That probably finally made your parents happy, then."

"Maman was very proud. When I bought my first house, I moved her in with me and she was by my side for the rest of her life."

"What about your dad?"

Maziar became sullen, "Baba…he was never able to… accept what happened."

"You dropping out?"

"No, no. Baba was...a proud man. All his life, he knew he was meant to serve his country. So, when he lost that and saw what they were turning his country into, you know…" Maziar played with his food. "He refused to get a job here. '*We will go home soon,*' he'd say. Maman and my sister supported him while he pissed away every cent they came here with. Eventually, he drank himself to death, and that was that."

Maziar drank the rest of his wine and retreated into his own memories for a moment. Then, he re-emerged with a smile.

"Sorry, I didn't mean to get so morbid, my God—"

"It's all good, man. I'm sorry for interrogating you."

"Oh, that's okay."

"I just like hearing stories from, y'know, people who came here from there."

"No, please, thank you for asking. How else are we going to keep these people's memories alive?"

"Right, yeah. That was actually the idea behind the book I'm working on right now."

Lisa gasped, "*Cyrus*, I didn't know you were an author!"

"I've had a few books published."

"No way! I will order all of them, but only if you promise to sign them."

"So, we have a celebrity sitting at our table," said Maziar.

"I wouldn't say I'm a celebrity."

"Do you have a Wikipedia page?"

"Yeah."

"Then you're a celebrity. *Hala* what's your new book about?"

Cyrus sat up proudly, "Well, my parents are still with us—thank God—but they're getting older, y'know? So, one day I started asking them to tell me stories about growing up in Iran and I'd record them. Just for myself, really. But these stories were just so amazing and I learned so much about them, and then I realized...there's like, a whole generation of immigrants who have stories like this, but for whatever reason they never get to tell them. So, my book is just a collection of stories from immigrants, not just from Iran, but all over the place."

"I'd be happy to tell you some stories, if you're still looking for people."

"Mazi has a lot of great stories."

"Oh, I'd love to."

"That's so exciting, Mazi!"

"Where do I sign?"

"He can't have one friend without it being a business relationship in some way."

"What are friends if they don't help each other get ahead in life? *Dammet garm, Koorosh-jaan*, I'll help you in any way I can."

"You know who you can also interview, Cyrus? Antonio, our chef."

"Oh, yeah?"

"He came here from the Philippines only ten years ago and he's told me some wonderful stories."

"I'll do it in exchange for that lumpia recipe."

"No, but really, that's another person who came here with nothing—and I mean literally nothing—and all he had were these recipes in his head that were passed down in his family for generations, and he made a great life for himself. He's got a *husband* now, and they just adopted a little girl from his home country. It's just the most beautiful story."

"Have you tell Sam this story?" asked Shireen.

"Sam? No, I don't think so."

"Why would we tell Sam?" Maziar asked with a slight defensiveness in his tone.

"I ask because I think actually it would be good to someone like Sam to hear this."

Maziar was taken aback, "*Someone like Sam?*"

"Someone who...may not know how...difficult it is for someone to come to a new country."

"He already knows."

"Mazi's always been very open about his journey as an immigrant."

"I tell him all the time because I don't want him to take this life he has for granted."

"But...I understand...but when someone is mean or, ehh, prejudice, I think it is because...a lot of the time, they don't understand other people's experience."

"I get what she means," said Cyrus. "She's saying maybe if Sam could walk in the shoes of recent immigrants like Parham—"

"I see where you're coming from. Really, I do. But, as we said before, Sam has learned a lot from all this."

"He has," Lisa nodded.

"And also, I think it can ultimately be a positive thing for Parham too."

Lisa turned to Maziar. Even she couldn't get behind that.

Shireen set her utensils down, "What's positive?"

"Well, when you tell me about your boy, you know who I think about? I think about my younger self. I was a little bit older than him, sure, but I was here in a time when you didn't see a lot of people who looked and sounded like me. So, I was an easy target. But what that gave me was a desire to work twice as hard as everyone else—"

"Parham *hameesheh* worked hard."

"*Meedoonam, azizeh delam*, but believe me when I say your Parham already has a big advantage over the American kids his age because of how much he struggles right now."

"How that would be advantage?"

"It's just what I see with Sam and kids is age is that they seem to be like, allergic to struggle."

"I dunno if I agree with that," said Cyrus.

"Uh-oh, are we back to arguing, gentlemen?"

"No, we can disagree without arguing, right? We're adults."

"We can. So, *Koorosh-jaan*, why do you disagree with me?"

"Well, I think—"

Maziar grabbed a knife, "GET THE FUCK OUT!"

Shireen jumped in her seat, knocking over Cyrus' wine glass.

Maziar immediately dropped the knife, "*Azizam, bebakhsheed*, it was just a joke."

Cyrus rubbed Shireen's shoulder, "He was just joking, babe."

"I'm sorry. I clean this," Shireen sputtered as she scrambled to wipe the red mess with a pile of napkins.

Lisa took the napkins from her, "Oh, honey, it's okay. Don't worry about that."

"Sorry."

"Don't apologize, sweetie. My husband just has a sick sense of humor."

"And is a very good actor, apparently."

Lisa hit his arm.

"Okay, sorry. Are you okay, *azizam?*"

Shireen nodded.

"She's okay. Everybody, relax. Sit down. Again, I'm very sorry. *Koorosh*, you can continue with what you were saying."

"No murder tonight?"

"No murder. I promise."

Cyrus took a breath to gather his thoughts, "What I was gonna say was...from my point-of-view as—I guess, what they call an older millennial, who works with kids every day—I think these kids do face a unique set of struggles that you and I never had to."

"They're in university, aren't they? How many of their parents had that opportunity?"

"I'm not talking about opportunity. Sure, this generation has more opportunities than—"

"But my point is, you cannot have success without failure. I'm talking about miserable, fall-on-your-ass *failure*."

"But, like, haven't we failed these kids enough?"

"You're absolutely right. We have failed them and that's the problem. We fail them every time we let them take the easy way out and not face their problems. That's what they're teaching them now in these schools and it breaks my heart."

"I wouldn't say that."

"I've seen it myself. When Sam was going to public school, he comes home one day wearing nail polish—"

"He let a girl he had a crush on paint his nails."

"I go to his teacher the next day and I ask, 'How can you allow this in your class?' The guy tells me it's not a big deal."

"It wasn't a big deal, but we're not gonna have this argument again—"

"He tells me the kids are encouraged to express themselves however they want. Not just allowed, but *encouraged!*"

"Why's that a bad thing?"

"Please don't get him started, Cyrus."

"Okay, long story short, I put him in private Catholic school from then on. We're not religious, but at least over there, they won't encourage kids to wear nail polish and identify as cats or whatever—"

Cyrus threw his hands up, "*Ooo-kay*, I dunno if I can go there with you."

"Oh, I forgot, you'll probably get fired for even thinking this stuff."

"Anyone want more *khoresht?*"

"Look at him. He's sweating."

"Oh, Mazi, leave him alone."

"*Koorosh, azizam*, relax. Your students aren't listening. In this house, we can speak our minds about anything."

"And my mind's telling me there's nothing I can add to this particular conversation."

"I can tell you're sick of it too. Blink once for 'yes.'"

"Mazi, enough."

Maziar turned to Shireen, "All this stuff must have been a real culture shock for you."

"I don't…"

"All this…*pronoun, mronoun* stuff."

"Sorry, I could not follow what you were talking about."

"*Heechee*, we were just talking about all the kids nowadays who mutilate themselves and change their genders and expect the rest of us to think it's normal."

"And you think this is...shocking for me?"

"Oh, it must be. *Oonjah een khabaraah neest*. You've never seen a man go up to a *basiji* and say he's a woman, have you?"

Shireen had to stop herself from laughing, "I mean…what was the song lyric? 'Because of the girl who wished she was a boy.'"

"But that means something completely different. He's saying the girl wished she was a boy because boys in Iran have more freedom."

Cyrus chimed in, "I also read it as a trans thing, albeit, a little reductive, but his heart's in the right place—"

"What are you guys talking about?" Lisa asked.

"She's just quoting me irrelevant song lyrics to prove her point."

"Okay, but...we have people like that in Iran also. Is just over here, you know, the government don't kill them for it."

"They sure do try though," Cyrus remarked under his breath.

Maziar leaned back in his chair, "I suppose it's better that people can live as they choose here. Let me clarify: What adults do to their own bodies, that's their business. But when they try to change the way I speak, or when they bring children into it, that is where I draw the line. Is keeping some basic decency not reasonable?"

Lisa nodded, "With children, it's perfectly reasonable. I don't...I have several *wonderful* queer friends, and I bet even they would tell you a child is not ready to make that kind of life-altering decision so early."

"Yes, to go back to what I was saying, every one of us has struggled with identity in some way or another. To a young person, struggle is a good thing because that's how they learn who they really are."

"And you're saying these people don't struggle?" asked Cyrus.

"When they're so easily allowed to legally and medically change their identities, no. That's the opposite."

"Guess we're just gonna have to agree to disagree there."

Lisa jumped at the opportunity to change the subject, "Yes, let's do that. There's a reason they say don't discuss politics at the dinner table."

"We were having a nice conversation before all that."

"Yes, what was it?"

"Uh, immigrants."

"Right. Immigrants. Good only if they're legal!"

Cyrus and Lisa burst out laughing.

"Okay, no more wine for you, Mazi."

Ding. Maziar received a text message.

"What is it?"

Maziar imitated a teenage boy, "*Bring food.*"

"Want me to take it up to him?"

"I'll do it."

8

It was mostly on a whim.

A combination of impulse, boredom, and genuine curiosity. Maziar had nothing better to do. He would join his guests downstairs shortly. But for now, he was stuck on the toilet in yet another bitter battle against constipation. It wasn't going to get the better of him tonight. He could feel it coming out.

So, in the meantime, he pulled out his phone.

He typed the name *"Cyrus Ghorbani"* into a search engine, eager to learn a little more about the man downstairs.

***

Cyrus admired the Lion and Sun painting.

"Did you paint this one too?"

"This? No, it was commissioned. One of Mazi's clients has a son who's a really talented artist and he painted this for us."

"It's beautiful."

"Thank you, yeah. I like it quite a bit. Very…opulent."

"Know the history behind it?"

"It used to be on your national flag, right?"

"But do you know why?"

"Not really, no."

"Wanna learn some history?"

"*Oooh*, of course."

Cyrus sat up and rubbed his hands together, "I can finally put the degree to good use."

Lisa poured herself another glass of wine, ready for his lecture.

"So, at first, the Lion and Sun had more of a secular, astrological meaning behind it—quite literally, the sun in the house of Leo. So, no religious or even national connotation. That is, until the latter chunk of the Safavid era—the Safavid Empire being the major empire that ruled after the Arab conquest that brought Islam to Persia—where the symbol makes a big comeback with the lion looking a little different, and the sun having a human face, and this was basically to represent the two pillars of society at the time: state and Shi'a Islam, because to them, a shah was both ruler and holy man. Later on—and I know, I'm skipping over a lot—the Qajar dynasty comes around, and for a while, the symbol still more or less stands for state and religion. But then, when the next two Qajar shahs take over, the lion gets a sword, and the sun loses its face because now, the sun represents the king of the motherland, and the lion is now a symbol of protecting your country against enemies. That's because during this time, we start to see the Islamic component of Iranian identity de-emphasized in favor of something more nationalistic. In a sense, the Qajars considered their Lion and Sun a symbol of sovereignty from colonial rule—both Islamic and European—and a return to their pre-Islamic roots. Same goes for the Pahlavi dynasty, who gave their lion a shiny new crown. Now, a common misconception you'll hear is that the Lion and Sun specifically belonged to the Pahlavi dynasty, which was why after the Revolution of seventy-nine, it was seen as a symbol of so-called 'Westernization,' so it was replaced with what we have now, which is a stylized spelling of the word, 'Allah.'"

***

Maziar tapped on Cyrus' Wikipedia page.

The main image was of Cyrus holding an award next to a banner that read "*PAAC: Persian American Action Committee.*"

He tapped on the image to make it larger, then zoomed into the banner.

The color drained from Maziar's face.

9

United States District Court, District of Columbia

Dr. Parsa Hafezi and PERSIAN AMERICAN ACTION
COMMITTEE
(Plaintiffs)
vs.
Hamid Sadeghi
(Defendant)

Memorandum Summary (abridged)
PETER BAUMAN, District Judge

This is a defamation case filed by Dr. Parsa
Hafezi and Persian American Action Committee
(abbreviated as "PAAC"). Plaintiffs allege that
Hamid Sadeghi published numerous false and
defamatory statements that characterize

Plaintiffs as paid agents of the Islamic Republic of Iran.

Dr. Hafezi is the president of PAAC, a Washington, D.C.-based non-profit group that "seeks to amplify and represent Iranian-American voices in the American political sphere." Mr. Sadeghi is a Florida resident who published articles about Dr. Hafezi and PAAC on various websites and his own personal blog. Plaintiffs' complaint seeks damages and injunctive relief against Defendant for common law defamation and portrayal in a false light. Plaintiffs allege that Defendant's statements injured their reputation amongst the Iranian-American community and hampered their ability to raise public funds by indicating that Plaintiffs are "members of a subversive and illegal Iranian lobby colluding with the Islamic Republic of Iran."

The Court has previously held that PAAC and Dr. Hafezi are limited public figures. As such, they had to have shown clear evidence that Defendant's statements were made with "actual malice" in order to prevail on their claims. To establish actual malice, Plaintiffs must show evidence that Defendant knew that the challenged statements were false. Subjective ill-will does not establish actual malice, nor does malevolent motive for publication.

The Court has found that Plaintiffs have failed to define the universe of allegedly defamatory statements. Plaintiffs have attached several articles, but have for the most part failed to identify which statements they perceive as defamatory.

For example, Plaintiffs protest that Defendant accused PAAC and Dr. Hafezi of refusing to speak up on and publicly condemn human rights abuses in Iran despite evidence that Plaintiffs had in fact done so. However, Plaintiffs put forth no evidence to that Defendant ever saw the statements related to human rights that are cited in Plaintiffs' affidavit. Furthermore, many of the statements listed in the affidavit are not as strongly and unquestionably anti-regime as Plaintiffs claim. One such statement of Dr. Hafezi's that Defendant criticized in his blog was the following:

> "I am not going to sit here and argue that Sepah [the Islamic Revolutionary Guard Corps] are not deserving of condemnation for their repeated crimes against innocent Iranians. They absolutely deserve to be condemned! All I'm saying is that it's incredibly insidious of Israel — a government with its fair share of well-documented human rights violations — to keep bringing up the Islamic Republic's treatment of Iranians as a means of scoring virtue points in the eyes of the international community."

That Dr. Hafezi occasionally made statements reflecting a balanced, shared-blame approach to the human rights crisis in Iran is not inconsistent with the idea that he was first and foremost an advocate for the regime. Given the other evidence Defendant amassed to support his views, the Court sees no "actual malice" in Defendant's decision to disregard occasional contrary statements and assume they were made largely to burnish Dr. Hafezi and PAAC's image in the United States. After all, any moderately intelligent agent for the Iranian regime would not want to be seen as unremittingly pro-regime, given the regime's reputation in the United States.

Although nothing in the Court's opinion should be construed as finding that the disputed statements in Defendant's writings were true, Defendant's motion for summary judgement will be granted, and all counts of Plaintiffs' complaint will be dismissed.

10

For a while, Maziar was quiet. Cyrus and Lisa, engaged in their conversation, barely noticed him return to the table. Shireen could sense something was wrong. Her ex-husband would have that same look whenever he came home from a stressful day at work or got off the phone with his mother. She had learned not to engage. So, she said nothing.

"Law school was the original plan, but then I took a couple gap years after undergrad and had a little identity crisis, and...yeah, pretty much overnight I decided I wanted to study the Middle East. To this day, I dunno what the thought process was. I just—"

"You heard a calling."

"Something like that, yeah."

"The universe can be like that sometimes. Like...I tell this story all the time, but my whole life, I was a hundred percent sure I did not want children. In fact, I was a hundred and *ten* percent sure. Cut to, I'm in my mid-twenties, working a job I hate at some pharmaceutical company, but at least I'm making good money and have enough free time to do everything I ever wanted to do. Then, one night, I had a dream where I was giving birth—like, actually giving birth for hours and I felt all the sensations and everything. Not once before or since then have I had a dream that vivid. The next day, guess who walks into my life."

"No way!"

"Right, Mazi?"

Maziar was still lost in his own thoughts.

"Everything okay, babe?"

Maziar snapped out of it, setting his sights on Cyrus.

"Does anyone want tea?"

***

Maziar always prepared his Persian tea with care. He had an electric kettle, which he would use for his other teas. But for his Persian tea, he would use a samovar, an urn-like metal container with a tap near its base and a chimney in the middle. His mother had bought it secondhand when they first came to America. Back then, its gold plating made it shine from miles away. Now, it was a big, archaic copper contraption with ever-peeling patches of discolored gold here and there.

He filled the bottom compartment with water and placed charcoal from his barbecue in the central chimney. As the lit charcoal boiled the water, he measured loose tea leaves—one teaspoon per cup of tea and not a single leaf more—into his porcelain teapot. Once the water in the samovar boiled, he poured a small amount of it into the teapot. He swirled the hot water around in the teapot for a few seconds in order to rinse the tea leaves and prepare them for brewing, then poured it out. After rinsing, he gently filled the teapot with the rest of the hot water. He brewed the tea for six minutes because he liked his tea strong. It was now ready to serve to his guests.

***

In the backyard, one maid lit the patio fire pit while the other pulled the plastic covers off of the chairs around it.

***

A brief moment of privacy.

"It's getting late, no?" asked Shireen. By this point, she knew there was nothing more to be gained by staying.

"We'll leave soon. Let's just have our tea, then we'll head out."

11

Central Intelligence Agency
National Foreign Assessment Center
8 December 1978

INTELLIGENCE MEMORANDUM (abridged)
Subject: Iran: The Tudeh Party and the Communist
Movement

KEY POINTS

-The Tudeh Party, Iran's pro-Soviet Communist party, is deeply rooted and in the past has shown an ability to exploit grievances to achieve very rapid growth.

-The leaders of the Iranian Communists are in exile in East Europe, but could return to Iran in a matter of days if the situation permitted.

-Since the Tudeh Party was suppressed nearly 30 years ago, it has actively recruited students in Europe. It has also stressed the development of an efficient and disciplined organization within Iran.

-The Tudeh Party has followed pragmatic policies. It has for years emphasized cooperation with other opposition groups and, in contrast to Maoist offshoots, does not preach the use of violence against the government.

-We believe that an underground organization exists within Iran, but because of the small amount of evidence available we are unable to estimate the current size of the party.

-A few Tudeh Party organizers apparently surfaced during antigovernment demonstrations, but they do not appear to have been the leading force in fomenting disturbances. It is extremely difficult to distinguish Tudeh activities from members of other groups that use Marxist jarjon [sic].

-Since early September Communist leader Iraj Eskandari has applauded the Shah's secular and religious opponents and reiterated the Communists' willingness to participate in a united front.

-If the government collapses or restrictions on political activities are lifted, the Communists could make rapid gains because of their discipline and sense of purpose.

12

Cyrus laughed with Lisa as Maziar watched him from across the flames. The only one who could feel the tension was Shireen. But, she said nothing.

Maziar finally spoke, "Do you like my tea?"

"Oh, it's great. Reminds me of home."

"*Noosheh-jaanet*. I'm glad you like it. You can't get tea like this over here."

"This from Iran?"

"It is. My friends bring it for me because they know how much I like it. But...let me ask you something: When you were in Iran, did you drink tea?"

"No, actually. I didn't start liking it until kinda recently."

Lisa butted in, "That was actually me with pickles—"

"Growing up, I probably drank more tea than water. We would always buy our tea from the exact same family, who had been selling that exact same tea, at the exact same little shop for years. Hundred years, probably. After everything that happened to our city after we left, I figured that shop was no more. But, I was curious. Years later, one of my friends was going to Iran to see his dad. They lived in more-or-less the same area I grew up in, so, I asked my friend to go see if the little shop was still there. And it was."

"Wow, that's amazing," said Cyrus.

"He got me some tea and brought it back with him. I can't tell you how excited I was when I made it. Just the smell of it took me all the way back. And then I poured it, and I took the first sip."

Maziar sipped his tea, swirled it in his mouth, then swallowed.

"In that first sip, I was back to being a boy. The taste, the smell, *exactly* what I remembered. But then, I took another sip."

He took another sip.

"And another."

Then another.

"And another."

Then another.

"And with each sip, it tasted less and less like the tea I remembered. Don't get me wrong, it was still miles ahead of any tea I've had here, but something about it was different. I didn't know what. It didn't take long for me to finish the batch my friend brought over—each time trying, and failing to recapture what I tasted with that first sip. So, since then, I've always asked my friends to go to that little shop—if it's not too much trouble, of course—and get me that tea. And every single time, the taste is just a little bit off. My friends think I'm crazy, but I've narrowed it down to two theories. The first is water. The mineral composition of American water is different from Iranian water, so, I assume it interacts differently with the tea and gives it a different flavor. My second theory is this: Usually, tea is not the only thing you bring over from Iran, right? You've gotta bring *lavaashak*. You've gotta bring *zaferoon*. You've gotta bring *aajeel*. All these things have a smell. And no matter how many layers you wrap them in, if they are packed together in a suitcase, those smells will combine. What I think is, the smell of all these things may have affected the flavor of my tea. Barely noticeable, I know. But I notice it. Now, who am I to tell my friends to bring me water from Iran that will likely be taken away by customs, or dedicate a whole suitcase to a tea that they are already generous enough to go and buy for me as a souvenir? So, in order for me to once and for all see if this is indeed the same tea from my childhood, I would have to try it in Iran. But first, we must take our country back. And by the end of this year, we will."

Maziar took another sip of his tea, then set the cup down.

"I have another story for you, *Koorosh-jaan*. This one is about a twenty-two-year-old girl named Mahsa Amini. In September of last year, Mahsa went to Tehran with her family to visit her brother. While on the expressway, this girl was arrested for not wearing her hijab properly. About two hours after her arrest, her brother was told she had a heart attack and a seizure—"

Cyrus cut him off, "I already…know about this."

"Even *I* know this," Lisa remarked.

Maziar leaned toward Cyrus, "Do you believe this girl was murdered?"

"Of course."

"Then why are you with PAAC?"

Cyrus' brow furrowed as Maziar stared him down.

"Who said I was with PAAC?"

"What's PAAC?" Lisa asked.

"Are you not?"

"No."

"Then why are there pictures of you at a PAAC event?"

"Did you look me up?"

"What were you doing with PAAC?"

"They gave me some achievement award a few years ago."

"That's it?"

Cyrus laughed.

"Why are you laughing?"

"Did you just invite us over to interrogate me?"

"I have no idea what my husband is—"

"That's not why we invited you."

"Then what is this?"

"Just questions from a concerned citizen."

"Clearly you're trying to say something with these questions."

"Can someone please explain to me what's going on here?"

"Our guest here just happens to be associated with a lobbyist group that launders billions of dollars for the Islamic Republic—"

"Okay, first of all, that is not true—"

"—and whitewashes their crimes against the Iranian people."

"None of that is true, but I'm actually kinda glad you brought it up, because—"

"Why are you even arguing with him?" Shireen whispered to Cyrus in Farsi.

"Because he needs to hear this."

"You married this guy?"

"Look, I've only been to a couple of their events and I don't agree with everything they say, but some of those people, I consider my friends."

"What do you think about your husband's friends, Shireen?"

"He know what I think of them, but right now we are not talking about—"

"The way they've been treated with these absolutely baseless accusations is frankly disgusting."

"Nothing baseless about it, *pessar-jaan.*"

"Their children get death threats. Did you know that?"

"And they care so much about the lives of other people's children?"

"How 'bout you give me one shred of evidence instead of just regurgitating talking points?"

"So, it's just a coincidence that every single policy suggestion they produce is exactly what the mullahs want?"

"But that's not laundering money."

"I know you are a smart man, but smart people can be naïve."

"Still waiting on that evidence."

"The Iran Deal."

"Just saying 'the Iran Deal' isn't proof that these people are laundering money for the Iranian government!"

"But read between the lines!"

"Speculation is not evidence!"

"*Hala* listen to me for one second."

"Go ahead. *Befarmaaeed.*"

"As a lobby group with influence, PAAC helped to negotiate the Iran Deal, did they not?"

Shireen spoke up in Farsi, "We did not come here to talk about politics. We came here because of my son."

"But this has now become something bigger than your son," Maziar replied in Farsi.

"Since we're on the subject of learning tonight, this can be a teachable moment for Maziar."

"Whatever you say. Now, back to what I was asking, in the long-run, who do you think benefited most from the Iran Deal?"

"Again, I'm not debating the pros and cons of the Iran Deal because that's another—"

"But you can answer my question."

"As far as the Iran Deal goes, it was, in hindsight, a misguided attempt to nudge the Islamic Republic towards reform."

"You say 'in hindsight' as if it wasn't so obviously a bad deal even then."

"Well, at the time, they felt it was important to maintain a diplomatic relationship between Iran and the U.S."

"Important only to the mullahs and the people in their pockets, which I'm sorry to say, your friends are."

Cyrus opened his mouth to retort when Lisa interrupted, "Hold on. Everybody take a deep breath. Let's actually take a deep breath. Come on."

Lisa guided Cyrus and Maziar to take a deep breath, as if she were teaching a yoga class.

"So, I'm not gonna pretend I understood…really…any of that. But, this is obviously something the two of you disagree on."

"If your husband actually listened to me, he'd see we don't even disagree that much—"

"*B'ap!*" Lisa put up her hand. "From what I gather, the two of you fundamentally want the same thing. Am I right? You both want a free Iran."

Cyrus and Maziar glanced at each other, then half-heartedly nodded like a pair of children being scolded.

"Good. And what's the theme tonight? We…listen and…"

"Learn," Cyrus and Maziar said at the same time.

"That's right, listen and learn. So, here's what we're gonna do. I'm going to give the two of you, let's say two minutes to state your case without any interruption. Who wants to go first?"

Cyrus looked at Maziar, "Wanna flip a coin, or—"

"No, I'll go first because I don't need two minutes. These people claim to represent the Iranian-American community, and yet I don't know a single Iranian-American who has ever believed that making deals with these terrorist leaders will eventually lead to democracy in Iran. So, either your friends are just totally ignorant, or, they are being paid to be mouthpieces for said terrorist leaders."

"Those are the only possibilities?"

"*B'ap!*" Lisa's hand once again went up. "Are you finished, Mazi?"

Maziar simply leaned back and crossed his arms.

"I'll take that as a yes. Go ahead, Cyrus."

Cyrus took a breath, "I believe PAAC is—at worst—a very out-of-touch liberal think tank that still holds onto the idea of reform as the ultimate solution. They're wrong, but claiming they're money launderers without any evidence is—"

"So you're just arguing about my word choice?!"

"Let him speak, babe. You've already had your turn."

"These are people's lives you're affecting with the things you say!"

"They go to the White House and make excuses for everything those monsters are doing to your own people every day and you care about my choice of words?!"

"There are a million smarter, less conspicuous ways to launder money than doing it through a lobby group in DC!"

"Okay, I don't literally mean they're laundering money."

"Then what do you mean?"

"Whenever we try to do anything to sanction the mullahs for their human rights violations, these people stand in the way."

"Iran's economy is directly tied to the personal wealth of the folks running the regime—"

"Bingo! So why are you arguing with me?!"

"—so, there's no way to sanction them without also economically punishing the Iranian people."

"Those sanctions are the reason the people of Iran are finally standing up!"

This made Shireen sit up, "Do you think they need your sanctions to do that?"

"I say this with all due respect to brave young women like yourself: They desperately needed to be pushed."

Shireen's eyes went wide, "Pushed?"

"By crippling their economy and cutting off access to potentially life-saving medicine?"

"Yes! When people are poor and frustrated, what do they do? They take to the streets and they burn down the establishment!"

Shireen was fuming. But, she said nothing.

Cyrus, however, ran into the fire, "It's easy to say that from the comfort of your mansion in the Pacific Palisades, but these are human beings; they're not weapons."

"*Borro, baba, human beings!* They tried to do the same thing with us just a couple years ago. First, with their virus that destabilized our economy—"

"Are you being serious?"

"—and then with getting kids to start a revolution here and overthrow our government."

"What are you even talking about? What revolution?"

"The…what was his name? The guy. 'I can't breathe' guy."

"George Floyd?"

"Yes, Floyd."

"What does Iran have to do with George Floyd?"

"It was a conspiracy."

"You think George Floyd's murder was a conspiracy by the Iranian government?"

Lisa tittered, "He doesn't *actually* believe it's a conspiracy."

"Not just Iran," Maziar clarified. "China and Russia too. If, thank God, the police didn't step in and put an end to it, it would've been a revolution. The things I saw in those few weeks *beh khodaah* reminded me exactly of what was going on in Iran in the seventies."

"So, you believe COVID and Black Lives Matter were orchestrated by foreign governments."

"No he does not. That was not what he said—"

"Let me answer him," said Maziar. "I don't believe they were orchestrated in the sense that they created these things. But what they did do was they...used things like social media and their partnerships with American corporations to...add fuel to the fire."

"How so?"

"What I saw in the summer of twenty-twenty were young people—disillusioned by a pandemic that took their jobs—looking for an excuse to take their anger out on the system. So, when Floyd died, our enemies saw an opportunity: *divide and conquer.*"

"Hold on, babe, I personally don't think they were influenced by anyone. That movement was a long time coming in this country."

"Give me a break—"

"No, look. My mother marched in the sixties during the Civil Rights Movement, and a lot of those problems are the same problems African-Americans face today."

"You are crazy if you think nothing has changed for them after all these years."

"I'm saying it's completely understandable that all that frustration led to some of the things we saw. Now, do I think *rioting* was how Dr. King would've wanted them to go about it? No, but—"

"Do you know the Iranian government named a street 'Shaeed George Floyd?' Know what *Shaeed* means?"

"What does it mean?"

"It means martyr. Martyr George fucking Floyd!"

"That's nice."

"No! Imagine if over here they named a church 'Saint George Floyd.' You wouldn't call just anyone '*Shaeed*,' let alone that guy!"

"Well, it was probably an act of solidarity between two countries that—"

"*Bull-shit*, solidarity! They knew exactly what they were doing with a gesture like that!"

"But you think maybe they did that to take attention away from police brutality in Iran?" Cyrus asked.

Maziar clapped his hands, "*Baareekalaah!* Exactly that!"

"Lemme ask you this: Why do you think Iranians have resorted to looting and rioting?"

"Because they tried diplomacy and reform. It didn't work. They tried voting for a reformist president. It didn't work. They tried peacefully protesting for their basic rights. It didn't work. So, what else should they do?"

"Do you think it's okay for them to burn down businesses in their own communities?"

"They don't own anything anymore. Everything those businesses make eventually goes into the pockets of the regime."

"In other words, those businesses are an extension of their government, and so destroying them is an effective act of protest against the government."

"Yes."

"Okay," Cyrus thought he had Maziar right where he wanted him. "So now, try to see that from the point-of-view of a Black person living in this country."

"These are two very different things, my friend. Facing the consequences of your own stupid decisions is not the same thing as living under a dictatorship."

"But we're talking about hundreds of years of deeply ingrained systematic oppression."

"No, we're talking about entitlement. Real oppression is what you get when entitled people get their way. Look at Iran. All that whining about, 'Boo-hoo, so much wealth disparity and discrimination under the Shah, even though our economy is the best it had ever been and women have more rights than ever,' where did that get us?"

"I wouldn't say the revolutionaries got their way, exactly."

"Of course they didn't. They blamed the poor Shah for all their own problems and now everyone else is suffering along with them."

"It seems to me like you're framing the Iranian Revolution as a thoroughly left-wing movement."

"Wasn't it?"

"Initially, yeah more or less, but what you're leaving out is the part where it eventually got hijacked by the religious right-wing."

"Well, you know why? Because, for as long as I can remember, these regimes have known exactly how to manipulate the left."

"Can you clarify?"

"I'm sure you don't need me to tell you the role that that Western imperialism played in making Iran what it is now."

"I am aware."

"There are people in Iran—most of them your age—who… they are not very religious. In fact, they would even prefer a more secular government because it would align more with their leftist, liberal ideals. But these same people will *fight to their death* to keep things the way they are. Why do you think?"

"A leftist and a liberal are two different things."

"That was not what I asked."

"Because they're scared of change?"

"Not change, because remember, these were the same kinds of people who helped overthrow the Shah, *khodaah beeyaamorzesh.* So, how was an extremely conservative Muslim cleric able to get a bunch of democrats, communists and Marxists on his side? By uniting everyone under one common enemy: the West. He made them believe our Shah was a puppet of the West. Realistically, if he was, the West would have done everything in their power to protect him. But these people, who were so blinded by their anger over everything the West robbed them of, allowed themselves to believe it."

"Don't you think the Shah throwing them in jail and having them tortured also might've had something to do with that?"

"He did that because he was a forward-thinking man. He knew what would become of his country if he'd let them run free."

"Well, it sure made them angrier."

"It's not the only thing he—"

"He should've arrested more. Hell, he should've had them all killed. The communists, the Marxists, the Mujahideen, the mullahs. All of them. Firing squad."

Maziar pantomimed firing a machine gun at Cyrus and Shireen, then laughed. Tears formed in Shireen's eyes and she quickly turned her head away. Cyrus, however, was fascinated by the man in front of him. He felt a rush he hadn't felt in years.

"You actually believe that?" Cyrus asked with a glint in his eye.

"Hundred percent. We wouldn't be having this conversation if that happened."

"If the Shah hadn't had millions of people executed for their beliefs?"

"Okay, maybe not necessarily executed, but...let me put it this way...you might be too young for this, but do you remember just how...taboo the idea of communism or anything like that used to be here in America?"

"Sure."

"It wasn't like now where every teenager wants to be a communist. It was like the plague. You couldn't even say it. So, sure, the Shah had SAVAK and they would do their best to...let's say, *silence* opposition. But what I think he could have also done was the thing that made America come out on top during their own conflict with the Soviets: making anything even resembling communism absolutely unacceptable, even when it came to their foreign policy."

"That's a pretty wide net you're casting there. Like, what would you consider resembling communism? I want free healthcare. Does that resemble communism?"

"In a perfect democracy, all ideas should be allowed. But what about the ideas that stand against democracy? Against freedom?"

"I'm afraid I still don't get what you're trying to say."

"What I'm saying is, if SAVAK was a brutal secret police force, then what is the FBI? If what the Shah ran in those days was a dictatorship, then what is America?"

"So, you're saying there can't be total ideological freedom in a democracy."

"Yes. America used to understand this better than anyone."

"Used to?"

"Well, look at the sorts of things we allow now: socialism being taught in schools, disregard for human gender, bending over backwards for radical Islam..."

"How do we bend over backwards for radical Islam?"

"By choosing people like Ilhan Omar to represent us."

"She's a radical Muslim just because, what, she wears a headscarf?"

"She does nothing but apologize for terrorists. You think twenty years ago, they would've let that bitch anywhere near the White House?"

"*Mazi*, we don't call women that anymore."

"Okay, that 'B.'"

"But, Mazi, don't you think it's a good thing that now we're letting Muslim Americans have a voice in politics?"

"Muslim, yes, but wearing that ridiculous thing on her head and saying the things she does is a slap in the face to women like Shireen here, who sacrificed so much to run away and be free from that stuff."

Lisa looked at Shireen, "What do you think, honey?"

"What I think?"

"These guys haven't let you get a single word in all night. Frankly, I'm more interested in knowing what you think about all this."

They awaited Shireen's response as she contemplated.

"I have to use the bathroom."

"Oh. It's, uh...once you go inside, it's down the first hall, second door to your right."

Shireen stood up and went inside. Maziar watched her leave.

"She's quiet, but she seems like a smart girl."

"She is."

"Not sure what she's doing with a PAAC-y, but..." he chuckled. "I'm kidding."

"Ha-ha."

"But really, I hate to keep badgering you, but these people have mastered the art of...as the kids call it, 'gaslighting.'"

"I see."

"You're clearly a very curious person. And that's a good thing. All I'm saying is, ask your friends enough questions, and eventually, they will show you who they are. Trust me, you don't wanna be associated with them for long."

"You know what I'm wondering?" Lisa asked. "So, like, suppose the current regime or whatever gets overthrown. Then what happens?"

"Well, right now, the focus is on getting them out."

"I mean, she does raise a good point," said Cyrus.

"What the mullahs want is for us to disagree about these things so that we get distracted from throwing them out."

"I totally get that, man, but having a solid plan of leadership is important, otherwise what you end up with is a power vacuum and it's gonna turn into another Arab Spring."

Lisa threw her hands up, "Okay, y'know what? Forget I asked!"

"You hang around your PAAC friends too much, because these are the exact kind of divisive, fear-mongering things they say."

"I don't think it's fear-mongering to say, 'Hey, let's not be so shortsighted if we don't wanna end up in the same situation in another forty years.'"

"The people are smarter than that. That won't happen."

"You do agree that leadership is crucial though, right?"

"Yes, absolutely."

"So, isn't it concerning that so far, no one's been able to agree on a single leader?"

"No one agrees right now because...young people...what they're useful for is getting angry and raising chaos. For now, we need that in Iran. But when it comes time to decide what happens next..."

"They shouldn't get a say?"

"Well, we already saw what happens when the young revolutionaries get a say. That's how we got into this mess in the first place."

"Didn't you literally just say they're smarter than that?"

"Smart, but they still don't know what they want."

"And you do?"

"All I know is Prince Reza Pahlavi is as good a choice as any."

"You want the Shah's son?"

"It's not about what I want. It's about what's best for the country."

"You've been living *here* for almost half a century though. So has he."

"But we've never been anything other than Iranian."

"Still, shouldn't the people actually living there decide?"

"Not when there's so much at stake."

"I think they know what's at stake."

"If they did, then they would come together and make a solid decision. But they have shown that they won't. All they know is what they *don't* want, and that's still a valuable thing, don't get me wrong."

"Why do you think going back to a monarchy would be what's best for the country?"

"No one said anything about monarchy."

"You called him 'Prince' Reza Pahlavi."

"That's his official title."

"So he doesn't claim to be a monarch?"

"All he claims to be is a patriotic Iranian who has always advocated for a secular, representative democracy."

"But, like...to play devil's advocate for a moment here, what makes him qualified to run a country? He's never held office, has he?"

"No."

"He's never even held a real *job*, as far as I know."

"But he is a leader."

"How do you know."

"Because it's his destiny."

Cyrus let him sit with that for a couple seconds.

"I mean…doesn't that sound like monarchy?"

"Call it whatever you wanna call it. The fact is that under the Shah, Iran was the most free and democratic it had ever been."

"Sure, but that's not a high bar—"

"But, listen to me, even he didn't run it like a traditional monarchy. He was only called 'Shah' because that was a title that he inherited."

"He didn't necessarily run things like a capital 'D' democracy either though."

"So, you're saying it was worse than what they have now?"

"I didn't say that. When did I say that?"

"Then you admit the Shah was a better leader than the Islamic Republic."

"Yeah, in the sense that I admit getting my nails pulled out is a better form of torture than having my balls electrocuted."

Lisa grimaced, "Do they really do that over there?"

"They both did, actually."

"No they didn't. What do you know? Were you there?"

"I wasn't in Nazi Germany either but I know—"

"There he goes with the Nazis again! Look, you can't run a country with that many people and that much oil in it without some kind of iron fist."

"He was a paranoid, deeply insecure dictator who caused his own downfall by ignoring his advisors and the legitimate grievances his people."

"Interesting. Which book are you quoting to me right now?"

"He had a lot of good ideas, don't get me wrong. I just think it's dangerous to lionize the guy and romanticize that time—"

"Tell me this—"

"—because the implied message there is that if you're living under a brutal dictatorship, you should just appreciate what you have because it can always get worse."

"Just answer me this: If Iran was such a terrible place under the Shah, then why did your parents and millions of others only leave once he was gone?"

"Just because it got worse didn't mean it couldn't have gotten better."

"Well, it didn't."

"But it could have."

"I think I understand what Cyrus is saying. Sure, there are dictators who are quote-unquote *worse* than others, but at the end of the day, a dictator is a dictator."

"Thank you!"

"Not true. A dictatorship doesn't necessarily have to be a bad thing. "

"Okay, where are you going with *this?*" Cyrus chuckled.

"Look at the president of El Salvador right now; the guy Lisa has a crush on."

"I do not have a crush on him."

"Technically, a dictator, but if you see what he's done for his country and how he's dealt with the cartels—"

"Give him a few years and we'll see if you still feel that way."

"Democracy is a great thing. But it is the end; not the means. If you want to rebuild a country, it will be ugly at first because not everyone will be on board. The Shah did what he had to do for his time. So, Prince Reza Pahlavi—or whatever you wanna call him—he will also adapt to the times and run his country accordingly."

"And you think he'll be accepted with open arms?"

"Of course. Why wouldn't he be?"

"That's not what I've been hearing."

"What you've been hearing is propaganda, my friend."

"The people in Iran chanting 'Down with tyrant, be it a Mullah or a Shah,' that's propaganda?"

"What the Shah was trying to build was a nation that could stand on its own, like it did for thousands of years. He wanted to give us back our identity. Whether they know it or not, that is what every single person fighting for a free Iran wants above all else: a reason to proudly call themselves Iranian."

"How can a nation stand on its own when you relentlessly sanction it?"

"When the mullahs leave, the sanctions will stop."

"*Khaylee delet khosheh.* Why don't you pay a visit to one of the many other sovereign, prosperous nations we helped bring about through our humane sanctions?"

"Oh, so we should just continue giving the regime billions of dollars and hope for the best. Got it."

"You see, when you argue that the young people at the forefront of this movement in Iran shouldn't have a say in the future of their country—"

"I never said that. I said they shouldn't be the *only* ones to have a say."

"But that your say should matter more?"

Maziar fidgeted in his seat, "Look, this is not an appropriate conversation to be having right now, I've gotta be honest."

"Why not?"

"Because—I said it before—what we, as Iranians, need right now is *unity*."

"But don't you understand why it can be hard for some people to take the whole 'unity' angle seriously when you use language that excludes the political left from the conversation—"

"They excluded themselves by siding with our oppressors. For the sake of democracy, there can be no place for them in our new country."

"What do you mean by that?"

"What I mean is...when the time comes, they will be dealt with."

For once, Cyrus was speechless. Maziar stared right back at him, the flames reflecting off of his dark eyes.

13

Central Intelligence Agency
Office of National Estimates
15 August 1958

INTELLIGENCE MEMORANDUM (abridged)
Subject: Iran: Outlook for the Shah

The swift and brutal overthrow of the monarchy in Iraq shocked and frightened the Shah of Iran and may cause him to reappraise the future of his personal position and his program in Iran. We have no hard intelligence which indicates an attempt to overthrow the Shah's rule is imminent. Yet many reports from a variety of sources indicate that basic and widespread dissatisfaction with the regime has created an atmosphere in which a coup could occur at any time. If, however, the Shah took dramatic and forceful steps to reform the corrupt social, political, and economic system, he might be able to maintain his position for the next few years. We believe the Shah is unlikely on his own to take such dramatic actions. If he does not, we believe the regime will become ever more unpopular and vulnerable to overthrow.

During the past two years the Shah of Iran has succeeded in consolidating all power under his personal authority and today controls even the day-to-day functions of government. At the same time, his personal prestige has decreased sharply. He is criticized and blamed for the continuance of near feudal economic and social conditions in the country. In spite of the

Shah's well intentioned public pronouncements concerning social and economic reforms he is blamed for the fact that little of real significance has been accomplished.

Although a facade of representative government has been preserved it is regarded by the vast majority of politically conscious Iranians as a farce. Elections are strictly controlled, debate in the Majlis [the Iranian Parliament] is limited, and all real opposition elements are suppressed through arrests and censorship. Opportunities for political expression and responsibility have decreased markedly over the past two years. At the same time basic economic problems and grievances have been accentuated as the total wealth of the country has increased. It is the popular belief in Iran that the country's growing oil revenues have gone mainly to enrich the ruling class. Actually a sizeable [sic] proportion of these revenues have gone into the Plan Organization, but the results have fallen so far short of expectation that the political impact has been adverse. Wealth is concentrated in the hands of a small group. Only two percent of the land is owned by the peasants who work it. Eight percent of government tax revenues are from taxes which fall most heavily on the poor. Flagrant corruption continues throughout the government, and the predatory economic activities of the royal family, including those of the Shah himself, and of the Court circle evoke widespread resentment and disgust.

We believe the future of the Shah's rule in Iran is extremely uncertain. We believe the Shah can maintain his position only by taking steps which will convince the public that he is breaking with the ineffectual and corrupt methods of the past. Measures to demonstrate that he can be a forceful authoritarian might win the support of conservative elements, but might at the same time touch off an opposition revolt. On the other hand, if the Shah were to take forceful and determined steps to eliminate corruption in government, if he initiated economic reforms, and established at least the beginnings of genuine popular participation in the government, we believe there would be a fair chance of orderly political evolution. We believe it would be psychologically extremely difficult for the Shah to relinquish absolute control of the government and admit to political responsibilities elements which he is convinced seek his personal downfall. Furthermore, he also would have to carry through programs which would damage the special interests of the royal family, the court, and the ruling class. We believe the Shah will be extremely reluctant and hesitant to take such actions and would be likely to do so, if at all, only under heavy and continuing pressure from the US.

It is generally believed in Iran that the US is committed to the support of the Shah and has a high degree of influence, even control, over the Shah. It is further believed that the US has not pressed the Shah to institute political and social reforms. Furthermore, it is widely assumed that the US supports and finances the Iranian intelligence service, SAVAK, which worked against all groups opposing the government. For these reasons the presige [sic] and influence of the US have declined along with those of the Shah. Yet there remains much good will and respect for the US.

14

No matter how long Shireen stared at it, she couldn't believe it.

The style was unmistakable. It was exactly what she envisioned when her grandfather and her parents had described it to her, minus one glaring omission: the man in the fire. Where was the man in the fire? In the painting her family described, the harem of Qajar girls had thrown a man in the fire before dancing around it in glee. But in this painting—this worthless replica of a masterpiece that had endured in the minds of all those who were alive to experience it—there was no man in the fire. It made her blood boil.

Across the room, the screen door slid open.

"I feel like next time, I should put shock collars on these two and press a button whenever they start to talk politics."

"I enjoyed our conversation though. Maybe next time, I can invite some of my PAAC friends and—"

Maziar patted Cyrus' shoulder, "Okay, don't push it *deegeh*."

"Ready to start heading out, Shireen?"

"Why head out? It's still so early."

"I've got work tomorrow, and…"

Shireen turned to face Maziar, "You said this was your favorite painting, yes?"

"Yes."

"In the original painting, there was…a man in the fire. They throw a man in the fire. Did you take it out?"

"*I* took it out," said Lisa. "I…felt it was a little morbid."

"It looks better this way, to be honest. I don't mind it. The beauty of the piece, to me, has nothing to do with that."

"Do you know who draw it?"

"I don't remember the name."

Shireen got choked up, "My grandmother draw it."

"Your grandmother!" exclaimed Cyrus. "That's right, her grandmother was a painter."

"Really?"

"Yeah, pretty famous in the pre-Revolution days too, actually. She'd like, use the styles of old Persian art to make satirical commentaries about class and culture."

"Wow! Such a small world!"

"SAVAK arrested her for her paintings," Shireen said with her eyes on Maziar.

Maziar crossed his arms, "No one got arrested for paintings in those days."

"They accuse her of...conspiracy against the Shah. Her paintings was their evidence. They were banned and some of them were destroyed. She died in prison. They force my grandfather to tell the papers it was a heart attack."

"I'm sorry that happened."

"You're not sorry for anything."

Cyrus took Shireen's hand, "Okay, Shireen, let's…"

Shireen removed her hand from his grip.

"Are you upset about the painting, honey? I really had no idea—"

"Shut up."

"Hey, don't tell my wife to shut up!"

Shireen switched to Farsi, "All night I've had to listen to you say such insulting, belittling things about your own people, and then you expect me to believe you when you act so shocked when your son insults mine?"

"Our sons have nothing to do with what we were talking about."

"They have everything to do with it. When Sam looks at Parham, he does not see a brother; he sees someone who is below him. But why should he see him any other way when his father thinks the same of me?"

"If I see you that way, it's only because of how you're behaving."

"How I'm behaving?!"

Cyrus stepped in between them, "Let's go home."

"If only you knew how much you're like those mullahs you say you hate so much."

Maziar's face went red with fury, "You know nothing, *dokhtar!* Clearly you've forgotten what it was like to live under those animals!"

"But unlike you, I *lived* under those animals! When the people marched against the Shah, it was because they wanted a better future. But along the way, they allowed themselves to become convinced that the only path to a better future was not forward, but backwards. So, they ended up with a regime that was worse than anything they could have imagined; a regime that made them long for the illusion of freedom they at least had in the previous one. I know I should be in Iran right now, fighting for my home. *But I'm here.* I'm here because I believed coming to this country would mean my boy would have a better life than I had. But what I see tonight is a country that is slowly but surely headed in the same direction as the one I left. So, when the young people of Iran reject your plans for their future, don't think for a second that it's because they don't know what they want. They do. It's because they don't want another revolution hijacked by those who only want to return to the past. It's because they are not willing to settle for anything close to what we have settled for here."

Maziar smirked, "If you like the mullahs so much, why don't you go back?"

Shireen—knowing her message had fallen on deaf ears—stormed out of the house, leaving Cyrus in the middle of the crossfire of tension.

"Sorry. Thanks for dinner."

15

Central Intelligence Agency
Office of National Estimates
August 1978

INTELLIGENCE MEMORANDUM (abridged)
Subject: Iran After the Shah

<u>EPILOGUE</u>

This review of people, institutions, and forces that will play a role in the succession to the Iranian throne suffers from a lack of information at key points. Masses of paper are available, but with few exceptions the kind of detail necessary to suggest how people might act is lacking.

The web of influence possessed by key figures cannot be mapped with any certainty; the debts owed and the favors received are virtually unknown. Some things known to be true a decade ago have not been addressed since then.

If the passing of the Shah is viewed as a significant event for US policies in the region, a firmer grip on less tangible influences seems advisable. To what extent does the traditional loyalty to the concept of a monarchy as distinguished from a particular dynasty still hold true? To what extent do the urban masses in Tehran provide an exploitable tool to support or oppose a new government? What institutions are so dependent on royal patronage that they would collapse if this patronage were withdrawn? Much charitable activity, for example, is directly connected with the Royal Family. The true opinions of key

Iranians toward the monarch is scantily documented. We knew much more about their views 15 or 20 years ago when many of these Iranians discussed with American officials the position of the Shah, his strengths and weaknesses, and even doubts about the viability of the monarchy.

Caution suggests that in future years persons, institutions, and trends be looked at not only for their current significance but also for whatever impact they may have on the succession of Shah Reza Cyrus Pahlavi, third and perhaps last of his dynasty.

16

"You didn't have to be so rude to them. All I'm saying."

Any confidence that Shireen mustered up earlier had deflated by now. She simply rested her head against the car window and watched the moonlit trees whiz past.

"He's an asshole and pretty much a fascist. I get it. But the thing with people like him is they're rarely exposed to viewpoints contrary to the ones fed to them by algorithms. Remember how he was when we first went out to the backyard? He was so deep into this misinformation nonsense about PAAC that he was ready to slit my throat right there just for being associated with them. Now, imagine if I'd immediately gone on the offensive. What would that have accomplished? He'd just retreat back into his little echo chamber and—like Jon Stewart said—those views would only continue to metastasize. You know what 'metastasize' means, right? It means, like…grow and spread like a cancer. If that's a cancer, then think of discourse as chemo. Doesn't always work and it's painful and time-consuming, but it's a whole lot better than ignoring it and just hoping it goes away. I listened to what he had to say, then he listened to what I had to say. We understood each other a little more. At the end of the day, that was the whole point of going to dinner there, right? Just understanding each other a little more. Y'know, that's what we need more of in this country…"

Shireen let him drone on. He would stop eventually.

***

One maid put out the fire in the backyard while the other laid the plastic covers back over the chairs. It was their final duty of the night.

***

Parham was asleep. Shireen kissed his head, and closed the door softly.

***

The tension released in the form of a laugh that ambushed Maziar and Lisa as they brushed their teeth together. They spit toothpaste everywhere.

***

Cyrus sat on the edge of the bed, taking off his shoes and socks. In the bathroom behind him, Shireen brushed her teeth.

***

Maziar and Lisa slept soundly.

***

Shireen woke up an hour into her sleep with the realization that she had not packed Cyrus and Parham's lunch for the next day. She made sure not to wake Cyrus on her way out. She made two sandwiches. For Parham, turkey and provolone cheese with light mayonnaise, pickles, and thinly sliced tomatoes on white toast. For Cyrus, turkey and provolone cheese with dijon mustard, pickles, and tomatoes on whole grain toast with the crusts cut off. Once the sandwiches were packed, she stayed up the rest of the night watching a Turkish television drama on her iPad.

***

The next morning, the sun rose over the Pacific Palisades, its light glistening on the face of the ocean in the distance. Lisa took Sam to school earlier than usual. She had to make it to her new pilates class by nine. It was in an unfamiliar area. Better safe than sorry.

***

Instead of getting on his Peloton, Maziar decided to go for a jog. He hadn't jogged in a while, but it was a nice day. He made sure to not jog downhill. He had heard that jogging downhill would be bad for his knees. He had healthy knees for someone his age.

His neighborhood's combination of flat stretches and uphill challenges made for a satisfying cardio workout. He ended up on a trail that took him to an overlook with an unobstructed view of the ocean.

This was home.

***

One maid vacuumed while the other dusted every nook and cranny of the living room. It was their first duty of the day.

***

When Maziar returned from his jog, Antonio began preparing a vegetable omelette that his mother would make for him. It had become a favorite of Maziar's.

***

Shireen and Parham did not speak as she drove him to school. It was nothing unusual. They weren't morning people. She dropped him off and watched him disappear into the crowd of students he was becoming more and more indistinguishable from every day.

***

Maziar came downstairs after a shower. On his way to the kitchen, he stopped by the painting of the Qajar girls. He hadn't looked at it since the previous night's confrontation. He studied it. The girls. The flame between them.

He shrugged and walked away.

***

Shireen's nails had become jagged. On her way home, she stopped by the nail salon. A Chick-fil-A was having its grand opening nearby in a building that had been boarded up since being ransacked by rioters three summers ago. She walked into the nail salon without an appointment, and after a short wait, was seated and attended to by a manicurist she was unfamiliar with. As the

woman began massaging her hands, Shireen closed her eyes.

She thought of her parents. Her parents who were once full

of hope. Her parents who were once radicals. Her parents who

stopped talking about politics. Her parents who, despite

everything, had become comfortable. Not wealthy, but

comfortable. Her grandmother. Her grandmother of whom she had

only heard stories. Her grandmother who remained courageous

until her last breath. But what was the legacy of that courage? Her

grandfather. Her grandfather the bitter old man. Her grandfather

the brave, outspoken old man. Her grandfather whose constant

rants about both the current regime and the previous one drove a

wedge between himself and his children. His comfortable children.

His children who, in his eyes, were a disgrace to everything their

mother died for. His secular children who believed another

revolution and regime change would only further burn their

beloved country beyond recognition. His grandchildren. His

grandchildren's generation for whom he had hope until his last breath. What would he think of Shireen if he'd lived to see her flee her home instead of fighting to make it better for future generations? What would he think of her new home?

Before she knew it, Shireen's nails were smooth. Shorter, but smooth.

Before she knew it, Shireen was comfortable. For now, despite everything, that was all that mattered.

EPILOGUE

A Joint Charter of Minimum Demands
February 2023

To the noble and free people of Iran!

On the 44th anniversary of the 1979 Revolution, Iran is facing an economic, political and social crisis that has engulfed the country and a clear and achievable vision to end it is unimaginable within the existing political framework.

Therefore, the oppressed people of Iran, including freedom-loving and equality-seeking women and youths, have turned the streets of the cities across the country into the center of a historic and decisive struggle to end the existing inhumane situation. Despite the bloody repression by the government, they have not rested for a moment for the past five months.

The fundamental protests raised today by women, students, teachers, workers, activists, artists, writers and the oppressed people of Iran in general in various parts of the country, from Kurdistan to Sistan and Baluchistan, is a protest against misogyny, gender discrimination, endless economic insecurity, labor slavery, poverty, misery, class oppression, ethnic and religious oppression, and a revolution against every form of religious and non-religious tyranny that has been imposed over the past century.

These protests have emerged from the context of large and modern social movements and the rise of an invincible generation that is determined to put an end to the history of a hundred years of backwardness and marginalization of the ideal of a modern, prosperous and free society in Iran.

After the two great revolutions in Iran's modern history, the leading social movements, including the labor movement, the movement of teachers and pensioners, the movement for equality for women, students and youth, and the movement against the death penalty, etc., have had a historical and decisive influence in shaping the political, economic and social structure of the country.

Therefore, this movement aims to end forever the formation of any power from above and be the beginning of a social, modern and human revolution to free the people from all forms of oppression, discrimination, exploitation, tyranny, and dictatorship. We, the union and civic organizations and institutions that signed this charter, focusing on the unity and interconnection of the social movements and demands and focusing on the struggle to end the existing inhumane and destructive situation, consider the following minimum demands as the first steps to meet the demands of these fundamental protests.

The people of Iran consider that meeting these minimum demands is the only way to build a new, modern and humane society in the country, and we ask all the noble people who have freedom, equality, and liberation in their hearts, from factories to universities, schools, and neighborhoods to raise the flag of these minimum demands:

1) *Immediate and unconditional release of all political prisoners, prohibition of criminalizing political, union, and civil activities, and public trials for those responsible for suppressing popular protests.*

2) *Unconditional freedom of opinion, expression, thought, [political] parties, local and national trade unions, popular organizations, gatherings, strikes, marches, social networks and the media.*

3) *Immediate cancellation of the issuance and execution of any type of death penalty and retribution, and prohibition of any type of mental and physical torture.*

4) *Immediate and full equality of rights between women men in all political, economic, social, cultural and family spheres, unconditional abolition of discriminatory laws against sexual and gender relations and tendencies, recognition of the rainbow society LGBTQIA+, decriminalization of all gender relations and tendencies, unconditional adherence to all women's rights over their bodies and destiny and preventing patriarchal control.*

5) *Religion is a private matter of the individuals and should not interfere in the political, economic, social, and cultural destiny and laws of the country.*

6) *Ensure work safety, job security and an immediate increase in the salaries of workers, teachers and employees, whether they are still active or retired, with the*

7) *involvement and agreement of elected union representatives.*

8) *Abolish laws and any behavior based on ethnic or religious discrimination and oppression, establish appropriate supporting infrastructures as well as the fair and equal distribution of government resources for the growth of culture and art in all regions of the country and provide the necessary and equal facilities for the learning and teaching of all languages used in society.*

9) *Limit the influence of the government and grant people the right to interfere in local and national councils directly and permanently. Dismissing any government or non-government official by voters at any time should be among the voters' fundamental rights.*

10) *Confiscate the properties of the individuals and governmental, semi-governmental and private institutions that have taken the property and social wealth of the*

11) *Iranian people hostage through direct looting or government rent. The wealth obtained from these confiscations should be immediately used to modernize and reconstruct education, pension funds, the environment, and the needs of the regions and Iranians who have been deprived and had fewer facilities under the regimes of the Islamic Republic and the monarchy.*

12) *End environmental destruction, implement policies to revive the environmental infrastructure that has been destroyed over the past hundred years and publicize the natural areas that have been privatized (such as pastures, beaches, forests, and foothills), depriving the people's rights on them.*

13) *Prohibit children's work and provide their education, regardless of their families' economic and social status. Establish public welfare through unemployment insurance and strong social security systems for all the people who*

14) *are of the legal age to work or are unable to work. Additionally, provide free education and healthcare for all the people.*

15) *Normalize foreign relations at the highest levels with all the countries in the world, based on fair relations and mutual respect, ban the acquisition of nuclear weapons, and strive for world peace.*

In our opinion, the above minimum demands can be achieved immediately, given the country's potential and actual underground wealth, the presence of informed and capable people and a generation of young people who are motivated to enjoy a happy, free, and prosperous life.

Signed,

The Coordinating Council of Iran's Teachers Trade Unions
The Free Union of Iran Workers
The Union of Free Students
The Center for Human Rights Defenders
The Syndicate of Workers of Nishekar Heft Tepeh Company
The Organization Council of Oil Contractual Workers' Protests
Iran Cultural House (Khafa)

Bidarzani
The Call of Iranian Women
The Independent Voice of Ahvaz National Steel Group Workers
The Labor Rights Defenders Center
The Kermanshah Electric and Metal Workers' Union
The Coordination Committee to Help Create Labor Organizations
The Union of Pensioners
The Council of Pensioners of Iran
The Progressive Students Organization
The Council of Free-Thinking Students of Iran
The Alborz Province Painters' Syndicate
The Committee to Follow up on the Creation of Labor Organizations of Iran
The Council of Retirees of the Social Security Administration (BASTA)

*****

Woman, Life, Freedom

BUSY

Amin wondered why his father looked so old.

It hadn't been that long. A year, give or take a few months. There was also the occasional five-minute video call. Then again, his father would always hold the phone so close to his face that the gradual loss of what was left of his curly salt-and-pepper hair was never apparent. Pixelation was another culprit, obscuring spots and wrinkles that hadn't been there before. Was he sick? Stressed out? How stressful could retirement be? Was that just how a seventy-one-year-old Persian man was supposed to look?

Shit, Amin thought. *Is that how I'm gonna look when I'm seventy-one?*

Everyone would say they looked alike. Amin never saw it. He only saw in himself his mother's pale skin and aquiline nose. Her straight, light brown hair too. To him, his only unmistakable resemblance to his father was in the color of his eyes: a striking blend of blue and green which—combined with Amin's pale skin tone and brown hair—led to a lifelong suspicion of some kind of European lineage. His father would claim their eye color was actually due to his side of the family's roots in Loristan. On a number of occasions, Amin considered sending out his DNA sample to one of those websites in order to lay the mystery to rest. Procrastination always won out in the end.

By thirteen, Amin was already a little under six feet tall, his slender frame towering over his stocky, five-foot-five father. The smiling old man standing before him appeared even smaller. The imposing physique that had once made up for his short stature had now diminished. But his hairy hands were still huge. He reached the right one over to Amin's left cheek, his sausage-sized fingers practically enveloping that side of his face.

Hossein's calloused palm brushed up against his son's perfectly groomed beard. He spotted a handful of silver hairs here and there. More than last time. He made that same hand into a fist, affectionately imitating a slow-motion right hook to Amin's jaw. Amin didn't flinch.

"How is vork?"

Those were the first words out of Hossein's mouth. Amin shrugged, "Eh, y'know." That was enough for Hossein. He didn't expect a longer reply. Didn't want one either.

The auto repair shop behind them was suddenly flowing with cars and customers. Hossein took his Prius in right when it opened, knowing how busy it would be later in the day. It was a shattered taillight. He was in bed, in the middle of a dream when he woke up to the sound of someone hitting his parked car and speeding off. "It'll be done by three," he was told. He would have had to wait at least a couple days if he hadn't been friends with the man who owned the place. He had a few hours to kill. He made some phone calls to see if anyone wanted to grab breakfast or lunch while he waited. No one picked up.

He called his son.

"*Amin-jaan*, vaat are you doing today?"

Amin was in bed, his wilting penis in his hand from the morning masturbation session his father had just interrupted.

"Nothing. What's up?"

He really did have nothing to do that entire day. That was seldom the case. Work was usually what kept him from making the two-hour drive to see his father. That, as well as everything else that happened to fall under the vague umbrella term "busy." He was always too busy. He could have just said he was busy. He would do that sometimes. Sometimes, he just wouldn't feel like driving. He didn't feel like it that morning. But they were due for a get-together. It was as good a day as any.

They walked side-by-side to Amin's parked BMW 5-Series. They were in no hurry. Hossein brought him up to speed on the latest family drama. Something about two of his aunts feuding over one of them recommending a dishonest pool cleaner to the other. Amin didn't listen to all of it. His mind was elsewhere.

"That's crazy."

Hossein hit his head on his way inside. The passenger seat was all the way forward.

"Shit, sorry," Amin muttered.

He reached over to help pull back the seat. Hossein already figured it out.

"You okay, Baba?"

Hossein nodded.

"You sure? You've got a little…"

"*Heechee neest,*" Hossein barked, rubbing the newly formed bruise on his forehead as if he could wipe it away. Amin knew better than to probe further. He started the car. The podcast he'd been listening to on the way there startled them both. Amin quickly paused it.

"Sorry."

They'd already run out of things to catch up on by the time they got to the diner. It was a cozy, retro-looking spot not far from the auto shop. They'd been there once before. Neither of them remembered. They took a booth near a window, not that there was any view worth seeing, but it was better than being in the middle. Not even two minutes had passed before Hossein began to mutter his complaints about the slow service. This would have normally led to bickering between the two, with Amin defending the overworked waitstaff and Hossein insisting on the laziness of today's workforce. This time, Amin pulled out his phone and checked his emails, ignoring his father's petty grumbles.

A waitress came to their table. Much to Amin's relief, she was an attractive young woman, no older than twenty-two. This meant that Hossein wouldn't voice his grievances to her and embarrass him. Instead, he'd flirt with her for longer than they had to wait for her to show up in the first place. Still embarrassing, but not nearly as much as it could have been.

Hossein read her crooked name tag, "Pilar. Beautiful name. Ver is your family from?"

"Thank you. We're from all over the place," she replied with her annoyance hidden behind a warm smile.

"Pilar is, eh…Mexican name, no?"

"I was actually named after my Argentinian grandma."

"Argentina! Most beautiful place I been. I love Argentina!"

He'd never been to Argentina. The only thing he knew about the place was their national football team. Fortunately for his white lie, she'd never traveled there either. He asked her if she knew how to make any good Argentinian dishes. She gave him the rundown of a provoleta recipe her grandmother had taught her, along with its chimichurri topping.

Amin was impressed by how convincing this woman was in playing along with his father. Of course, she had the same annoyed, tired eyes as all the other ones. It's hard to hide that. But her voice and body language remained inviting. Interested, even. Not that it mattered either way to Hossein. He was always oblivious to their utter disinterest in talking to him. Pretended to be, anyway. When Amin was in his teens and twenties, Hossein would involve him in the flirtation in an attempt to live vicariously through him. "This is my son," he'd say proudly. Nothing would ever come of these forced introductions, as far as Amin's romantic life was concerned. At some point, Hossein gave up. Granted, he never had any luck with the waitresses either, but at least he could get his kicks without his son's shyness ruining the fun.

Once the conversation reached its natural conclusion, the waitress managed to finally take their orders. A cafe latte and an egg, ham, and cheese croissant for Hossein, and a hot matcha tea latte with oat milk for Amin. Hossein leaned toward her, "Thank you very much, Pilar."

Her smile went away as soon as she turned away from them. Hossein stared at her behind as she headed for the kitchen.

"You should find yourself a girl like that," he said in Farsi.

Amin snorted, "Okay."

A mostly silent twenty minutes later, a server arrived with their orders. This time, a young man. Amin cringed even before Hossein started berating the man for the inexcusably long wait. Their drinks were almost tepid by the time the visibly shaken server left their table.

Before taking his first bite, Hossein tore off an end of his croissant and set it on a napkin in front of Amin. Amin slid the piece back to him.

"Vhy? It's good."

"I don't eat eggs anymore. Trying this new vegan thing."

Hossein furrowed his brow. *"Borro, baba. Bokhor deegeh.* Nothing going to happen," he insisted as he pushed the piece back in Amin's direction. Amin had to turn it down three more times before Hossein conceded.

They didn't talk much after that. They leaned back in their chairs, lost in social media rabbit holes as they slowly finished their drinks. Once they were done, the waitress arrived with their check. Hossein came alive again, "Thank you, Pilar. You have been vonderful."

They argued over the bill, as usual. Hossein would win every time. This time, Amin didn't put up much of a fight.

***

The day was starting to warm up. They had a few more hours. Amin suggested a movie, but Hossein wasn't in the mood. There was a park trail nearby that Hossein would frequent. At a leisurely pace, one could complete it in just over three hours. Good enough.

Hossein led the way. Despite his huffing and puffing, he could still out-walk his son. For an hour or so, there was nothing but the sounds of their breaths, their shoes brushing against the dry grass, and the various birds that were scattered all over the place. Amin's phone would also occasionally buzz with notifications from a co-worker group chat. He checked it from time to time. Nothing all that important.

Hossein finally broke the comfortable silence. "Vaat you think?"

"It's nice."

That was it for another forty minutes. Amin was exhausted. He stopped walking to catch his breath.

"Vhy you estop?"

Amin pretended to admire the grazing mallards. "Can we feed them?"

"No. There is more in the lake. Come." Hossein kept moving. Amin took three more seconds to rest, then followed him.

The lake was, indeed, filled with mallards. It was utilitarian, much like the park surrounding it. Not the cleanest or most beautiful sight in the world, but just aesthetically pleasing enough to provide the backdrop for a quiet picnic. That day, there wasn't another person in sight. Amin and Hossein found a bench overlooking the lake. Amin caught up on the group chat. Hossein leaned back, somehow finding something to admire in the view he'd seen countless times before.

After a few minutes, Amin yawned, "Wanna go?"

Hossein nodded. They got up and went on their way.

***

They arrived back at the repair shop right on time.

"Want me to wait for you in case it's not ready?" Amin asked.

Hossein unfastened his seatbelt. "No, is okay. You should go. Avoid rush hour."

He opened the door and gripped Amin's right arm.

"See you soon, *pessaram*."

"Later, Baba."

Hossein let go and stepped out.

***

Hossein's odor lingered on the drive back. It was a particularly pungent mixture of Tommy Bahama cologne and his natural, spice-like scent combined with dried sweat from all the walking. Amin found it nauseating.

He never opened a window.

TIMESHARE

"A second of your time? They told me to track down the best-looking couple here."

Yasmin blushed. Farhad remained stone-faced at the man's flattery. Still, they both found themselves drawn to his kiosk for one reason or another, shade being a major one.

He was a young man. Twenty-five, twenty-six. No older than their daughter. He started with small talk. "It's a hot one today," and "How're y'all enjoying the fair so far?" and things of that nature. Then, he got down to business.

"You've heard of timeshares, right?"

"Yes. Not interested."

"Don't worry. I'm not a salesman. You guys local, or are you on vacation?"

"Local."

"But first time coming here," said Yasmin.

The man shifted his focus to Yasmin, recognizing her as the talker of the two. "Do you travel often?"

"Hmm, not—"

"We travel when we can."

"And what's holding you back from traveling more?"

"My husband," Yasmin chuckled.

"Too expensive."

"I feel that. But what if traveling was free? Would you travel?"

Farhad shrugged, "Maybe."

"I see you've got a nice Hawaiian shirt on. How does a three-day, all-inclusive stay in Hawai'i sound?"

"For free?"

"For free."

"But only if I buy a timeshare, right?"

"Nope," the man said as he pulled up his tablet. "Again, I'm not a salesman. Frankly, *I* wouldn't be caught dead in a timeshare. Have either of you ever been to a timeshare pitch?"

They shook their heads.

"Perfect. So, here's how it works: You let them pitch their timeshare to you, and whether or not you end up buying, they offer you a vacation incentive at the end just for showing up."

"But what's the catch?"

"The catch is you've gotta sit through a timeshare pitch."

"We sit through the pitch, say no, and they just give us a free vacation to Hawai'i?"

"Trust me, with how much these timeshare companies rip people off, they can afford to throw money away just getting folks to show up to a pitch. I get paid just for signing you up."

Farhad and Yasmin glanced at each other. Without saying a word, they had a whole conversation.

"How do we guarantee they'll give us the vacation?" Farhad asked the man.

"They give you a voucher that covers both the flight and the accommodation. It's from a legit travel agency. You can call them and verify it if you want. I've done it myself before I started working for them. Took my girl to Catalina Island for a weekend."

"Where do we have to go?"

"Not far. Are you interested?"

"Sure. Why not?"

***

They stayed at the fair a bit longer until they ran out of things to do and bizarre culinary concoctions to try and throw away after a couple bites. It was getting too crowded anyway.

***

The resort was a twenty-minute drive away. It was on a hill, secluded from the city below. Families and couples hung out by the pool. A chatty elderly woman in a golf cart picked Yasmin and Farhad up from the parking lot and drove them to the main lobby, where they were told to check in and wait for Bobby. They checked in and waited for Bobby. Refreshments were available. Farhad stuffed bags of chips and nuts into Yasmin's purse, then poured two cups of coffee. Black for himself, and with a little bit of cream for Yasmin.

"Farhad?"

Their salesman was in his thirties. A bearded, dark-skinned, curly-haired man with bags under his eyes. He shook their hands.

"You guys Persian?"

"Yes."

"*Salaam, man Babak hastam,*" he said in broken Farsi.

As he took them on a long tour of the property and a couple of the rooms within it, he told them a little about himself. He was a first-year MBA student working in sales to help fund his education. He had a five-year-old son with his girlfriend. His father was Rashti and his mother was from Abadan.

After the tour, he took them to his office and had them answer some questions for a questionnaire.

"On a scale of one to ten, how important is traveling for you?"

"Two," Farhad leaned back in his chair and crossed his arms, wanting his demeanor to display nothing but disinterest as a way of telling Bobby to get on with it.

"Does the *khaanoom* feel the same way?" Bobby asked, setting his sights on Yasmin.

"Yes," Yasmin nodded. She knew he made money on commission and didn't want to waste his time. But at the same time, it was rude to be blunt about why they were really there.

"Not vacationers, huh?"

"No."

"What would you say is the main thing holding you back from vacationing?"

"No interest."

"Too much money," Yasmin added.

Mistake. Now Bobby had something to grab onto.

"I *totally* understand. Especially now, everywhere's so expensive. Like, last month, we took my son to Disneyland for his fifth birthday. He'd been wanting to go, and my girlfriend and I saved up for it and everything, and it still ended up costing an arm and a leg. Barely saw any families there either, and mind you, this was in the middle of the summer. Mostly a bunch of rich college kids. It's ridiculous."

"Even before everything got expensive though, we never traveled," said Farhad.

"You *never* traveled?"

"Here and there, sure."

"Here and there? You guys mostly stay local?"

"Yes."

"Like, where?"

"Like…San Diego."

"San Diego. I love San Diego. We actually have a beautiful resort up there, actually."

Farhad took a sip of coffee and checked his phone.

"On the form, you put down that you have a kid?" Bobby asked Yasmin.

"Yes."

"How old?"

"Twenty-five."

Before Bobby could ask further, Farhad cut in, "She's in college now. Doesn't live at home anymore."

"Nice, where does she go?"

"Washington State."

"Ah, cool. They're Cougars, right?"

Farhad shrugged, "Sure."

"So, what do you guys like to do for fun now that the kid's out of the house?"

"Not much."

"You don't do anything?"

"Not really."

"You just…stay home?"

"Pretty much."

"Why? Too expensive?"

"Sure."

"This guy doesn't take you on dates?" Bobby asked Yasmin.

"We…go, but…not too much."

"What does a perfect date look like for you?"

"Just…something simple and relaxed."

"Simple and relaxed, huh? So no big adventures, then."

"No."

Bobby slid the questionnaire to them along with his pen.

"From this list of cities and countries, circle which ones you're most interested in visiting. You can circle as many as you want to."

Farhad glanced at the list, "Not interested in any of these."

"None of them?"

"Nope."

"How 'bout you?"

Yasmin shook her head. Bobby was sweating now.

"Okay," Bobby said as he took the paper and pen back. "May I ask how old you two are?"

"We're in our fifties."

"You both look great."

"Thanks."

"Have you guys seen the movie *Up*?"

"The cartoon with the balloons?"

"Yeah."

"We've seen it."

"I showed it to my son the other day. First time he ever saw me cry. But it made me think. Know what it made me think about? Regret. Did you know the number one regret people have on their deathbeds is that they didn't travel enough?"

"That's unfortunate," said Farhad.

"You say money is the main thing holding you back from traveling. Totally understandable. I didn't grow up super well-off, but my parents always made sure to put some money aside for a yearly summer vacation. Nothing too fancy, but we never missed a year. I don't think my girlfriend and I can afford to go somewhere *every year*, but we agree it's important to travel. We think of it as an investment. Only what that investment yields isn't more money, but rather memories of *quality time*. That's our mission here. We want to give you the opportunity to invest—not just in property—but in yourself."

"I see."

"What interested you about timeshares?"

"Can I be honest?"

"Of course."

"We just came because they promised us a free trip to Hawai'i."

Farhad's bluntness did not make Bobby back down.

"I'm sorry, a free *what?*"

"Were we lied to?"

"No, a free…*what?*"

"A free trip. To Hawai'i."

"A trip? As in a *vacation?*"

Farhad was fed up, "We have no interest in buying a timeshare. I don't want to waste any more of your time. Please, just give us the voucher."

Bobby hid his disappointment behind a smile. "Very well," he stood up. "Thank you both for coming. I'll go get Linda. She handles all that stuff."

***

Farhad and Yasmin left the office with their voucher. They passed by Bobby in the lobby. He did not acknowledge them.

They drove home. Farhad put the voucher into a drawer in their nightstand. It remained there until their daughter found it as she was cleaning out their house and preparing it for sale.

WHOLESOME
RANCH MARKET

STARTED: December 11th 2022
POSTED BY: Abbas Ebrahimi
PETITION TO: Federal Bureau of Investigation

FBI please investigating WHOLESOME RANCH MARKET for possible Money Laundering w/ IRGC!!

I am a proud member of the Iranian American community of the United States! We are compromised of many hardworking and lawabiding individuals, and our community continues to be ranked among the highest educated immigrant communities living in this Great Country year after year. We make up for anywhere between 500,000 and ONE MILLION citizens who have made the United

States our beloved home, and what we value above all else is this country's committtment to freedom for all! This is why we believe it is the responsibility of our government to weed out any malicious individuals who are living and profiting among us while contributing to the persecution, torture, and muder of innocent Iranians abroad.

The Iranian regime is one of the most oppressive in the world and was rightfully designated a state sponsor of terrorism by the U.S. Department of State. It has committed serious and repeated human rights violations since 1979 and has the highest number of executions worldwide after China. It has a long history of cracking down on peaceful protests in the most vicious and inhumane manners, without any regards for the rights or wellbeing of its citizens. It is also one of the MOST CORRUPT and LEAST TRANSPARENT regimes in the world. In 2021, Transparency International's 2021 Corruption Perception Index ranked the Islamic Republic 150th out of 180 countries as perceived to have higher levels of public sector corruption. Iran's ranking has fallen steadily since a high of 130th in 2017. The CPI generally defines corruption as an "abuse of entrusted power for private gain."

Given the widespread corruption in Iran, the Iranian American community is gravely concerned that embezzled resources and funds have been transferred through the migration of people connected to the Iranian Regime to the United States. Many adult children and/or associates of the Iranian regime's current and former high ranking officials have successfully obtained visas, immigrated to the US, and established lavish lives and lucrative businesses in this country.

One such business, which has recently come to my attention, is Wholesome Ranch Market in Laguna Niguel, California. Wholesome Ranch Market is a popular Iranian supermarket in Southern California. For many, including myself and my family, it is a go-to place for ingredients for Iranian dishes, as well as other items that help us keep our wonderful culture alive here in America. Their kabobs (before they fired all their Iranian cooks and replaced them with Mexicans, that is) also were exceptional and a favorite of many people like myself. Therefore, it was at first difficult for me to believe it when I initially heard rumors within my community that the man who owned the store had an unsavory past. In fact, I refused to believe it! I continued shopping there because, for one thing, their deals were simply too good, and second, the only other Iranian supermarket close to us is in Irvine. That's a long drive for some groceries! So for a while, I said "To HELL with the rumors" and I was a loyal customer.

But all of that changed one day when I went shopping with my dear wife one day. I was in the refrigerated section looking for doogh (by the way it's another tragedy that they no longer carry Abali and have replaced it with some flavorless generic brand of doogh) when I heard something that put me in shock! I heard the song "Salaam Farmaandeh" playing. At first, I thought it was some idiot playing music on his phone too loud. But no. It was playing on the supermarket's radio system, much louder than normal, as if they WANTED their customers to hear it. As if they WANTED to make it clear where their loyalties lie at a time when so many Iranians all over the world are calling for regime change in Iran.

For my non-Iranian readers (or, like my kids, Iranian readers who grew up in America and are not in the loop), I will explain the song and its context. If you already are familiar with the song, feel free to skip over this paragraph. "Salaam Farmaandeh," or as I like to call it, the Mullah Bootlicking Anthem, is an Iranian song that was released earlier this year, just before the Persian New Year. Translating to English as "Hello, Commander," its lyrics pay tribute to Qasem Soleimani, general of the Islamic Revolutionary Guard Corps (IRGC) and a man with the blood of countless innocent Iranians on his hands. Back in 2020, Soleimani was turned into a kotlet courtesy of a drone strike ordered by President

Trump, much to the joy of Iranians like myself and the anger of other Iranians who support the regime. A member of the latter group decided to cash in on Soleimani's demise and make a song that aimed to highlight the new generation of Iranians supporting the Islamic Republic and its ideologies. This is why, if you watch (or rather, force yourself to sit through) the music video, there is heavy emphasis on young people singing along with the song. Some school choirs in Iran are even taught to sing the song, and back in May, it was performed at Azadi Stadium in Tehran. All of this is to say that there is no way anyone like myself would have this song on their playlist to just casually listen to it like it's Googoosh or something. There is no way to separate this song from its context. And, most importantly of all, there is NO WAY the people running Wholesome Ranch Market didn't know what they were doing when they decided to play this song loudly and proudly for their primarily Iranian customers.

From then on, I began looking into the store's history and listening closely to the whispers within my community. I slowly put all the pieces together. I discovered that the store's owner, Ali Eghbali, was a former member of the IRGC during and shortly after the Revolution. Despite having no formal education in business and being from a working-class background, he moved to Singapore in 1983 and, just two years later, opened a Persian restaurant there. The restaurant was, by all accounts, an upscale establishment with the finest of equipment and chefs imported from Europe. In other words, it was an expensive way to open a restaurant. Unreasonably expensive. And where did the funds come from? That part, one can only speculate about, but it is more than suspicious that someone like this would have the spending power to move to a new country and open a fancy restaurant within a couple years of moving there. That restaurant shut down by 1991, and a year later, Eghbali relocated to California. Again, keep in mind, this man spent loads of money on a failed restaurant, and yet still somehow had the funds to both buy a house in and open up a supermarket in Southern California within a year of moving there. Either Ali Eghbali is the greatest businessman in all of human history, or someone other than himself has been financing his operations. Wholesome Ranch Market has been operating since then, and as I said, has been a favorite among Iranians who live here. Eghbali himself has always remained tight-lipped about his political views. He has no social media and has rarely made public statements of any kind. Aside from informaiton that is already publicly available, it is difficult right now to look too deep into this man and those he surrounds himself with.

So, on behalf of the Iranian American community, I am respectfully asking the FBI to please begin investigating Ali Eghbali and the financial activities of Wholesome Ranch Market. It would be best if this investigation is started AS SOON AS POSSIBLE, given the ongoing human rights situation in Iran.

52,101 Signatures of 200,000

***

SUPERIOR COURT OF CALIFORNIA, County of ORANGE

DATE FILED: January 20th, 2023
PLAINTIFF: Ali Eghbali
DEFENDANT: Abbas Ebrahimi

Plaintiff requests temporary restraining order from Defendant that will apply to Plaintiff's home address as well as Plaintiff's business property Wholesome Ranch Market. Plaintiff alleges the following:

—Since December 4th of 2022, Defendant has been sticking flyers and posters with defamatory claims about Plaintiff on Plaintiff's place of business (pictures of flyers and screenshots of CCTV footage showing Defendant placing them have been attached to this document). This has resulted in the business losing regular customers.

—Defendant sent threatening emails to Plaintiff, as well as members of Plaintiff's family (screenshots attached to document).

—On January 16th of 2023, Defendant participated in a protest in front of Plaintiff's place of business, obstructing some traffic (corroborated by CCTV footage that is available upon request).

I, <u>Ali Eghbali</u>, declare under penalty of perjury under the laws of the State of California that the forgoing is true and correct.

***

THE ORANGE COUNTY REGISTER
2/5/2023

Local Businesses:
"A Piece of Home: Interview with Wholesome Ranch Market's Ali Eghbali"
by Dalia Ashouri

Southern California has become home to one of the largest Iranian communities living outside of Iran, with an estimated 32,000 of them living here in Orange County. My family is among them, and for as long as I can remember, we have been buying all of our groceries from one store and one store only: Wholesome Ranch Market (or, as my family calls it, "Maghaazeh Eeroonee"). Whether it's for kitchen staples such as dairy, fruit, and bread, or essential Persian spices and other traditional ingredients you wouldn't find at Ralphs, we have never felt the need to get our groceries anywhere else. Despite all the rapid growth and development in my hometown of Laguna Niguel, Wholesome Ranch Market has been open for business since 1993, right when Orange County was just beginning to become the Iranian-American hub it is now. The savvy, Iran-born businessman behind the store is Ali Eghbali, who for the first time ever, has agreed to sit down for an interview with the OC Register. I visited him and his wife Niloufar at their home in Laguna Beach. Our interview:

ME: First of all, Mr. Eghbali, thank you for allowing us to interview you. I have to admit, I feel a little starstruck. My mom told me to thank you on her behalf.

MR. EGHBALI: Well, the store would be nothing without the support of my wonderful community, so if Dalia's mom is reading this, I say, "Merci."

ME: The OC Register has reached out to you several times for an interview over the years, but you've always turned us down, so we were all surprised when you reached out and actually requested this interview.

MR. EGHBALI: I prefer to do these things on my own terms.

ME: So, why now?

MR. EGHBALI: Well, with what's currently going on in Iran, the Iranian-American community is having something of a moment in mainstream media right now. It was actually my wife who convinced me to do this interview, just to show the world the diversity of the Iranian-American experience. We're local businessmen, doctors, engineers, dentists, lawyers—hard workers that exemplify the American Dream.

ME: Speaking of the American Dream, tell us a little bit about your journey as an immigrant. I understand you were born in Iran.

MR. EGHBALI: That's right, I was born and raised in Tehran. Then, like many Iranian immigrants, I left Iran shortly after the Revolution in search of a new home. For a bit, that home was Singapore, where I dabbled in the restaurant business and failed miserably. Then, I followed some friends to Orange County, California. What I love about this country—especially in those days—is the ease with which someone can start a business. It's a country that puts business first, and wants businesses to succeed, even for an immigrant like myself.

ME: You opened Wholesome Ranch Market at a time when Laguna Niguel looked a lot less Iranian than it does now. Were they the customers you ultimately had in mind when you decided to open an Iranian supermarket?

MR. EGHBALI: I opened Wholesome Ranch Market, first and foremost, because I missed Iran and my family so deeply and I wanted to have just a little piece of my former home. I would always tell my non-Iranian friends about all the great food we had back home, and they'd tell me they wanted to try it. At first, the idea was to open another Persian restaurant. But I was still a little traumatized by my foray into the restaurant business back in Singapore, so I decided against that. Then, as I was grocery shopping one day, looking for ingredients that would just vaguely resemble fesenjoon [a Persian stew] ingredients, I had the idea of opening a supermarket specializing in Middle-Eastern products. So, at the end of the day, it was for selfish reasons (laughs).

ME: Do you have plans of expanding the store into a franchise? I'm sure there are a lot of other Iranian-American communities who'd love it.

MR. EGHBALI: Right before COVID, we were having discussions about it, but for now, I can't say anything definitive. I'm keeping my fingers crossed though.

ME: Lastly, can we address the controversy?

MR. EGHBALI: Yes, please, by all means.

ME: For readers who may not know, last month, there was a small gathering of protesters outside your store claiming that your business is actually some kind of money laundering front for the Islamic Republic of Iran.

MR. EGHBALI: (laughs and shakes his head) I'm sorry, it's still ridiculous no matter how many times I hear it.

ME: You've also filed for a restraining order against a local engineer named Abbas Ebrahimi, who was present at that protest. Do you know him personally?

MR. EGHBALI: No, I do not. By the way, as of giving this interview, I have yet to be granted that restraining order and my family is terrified. We've hired our own personal security team in the meantime. I have no idea what this man's problem with me is and I sincerely hope he gets the help he needs.

ME: What reason do you think he would have to make a serious allegation like that?

MR. EGHBALI: I really have no idea. Jealousy, perhaps? As you probably know, we Iranians can be petty sometimes (laughs).

ME: But, again, it's a very serious allegation.

MR. EGHBALI: I am aware of its seriousness, and it's something I take great offense to. To suggest that I—in any way, shape, or form—support those monsters who drove me out of my home country and oppress my people is the biggest insult you can possibly say to me. My wife's father served in the Shah's army. If I were an agent of the Iranian government, would they let me marry her? I created Wholesome Ranch Market with my own blood, sweat, and tears, so for this idiot to go around making these ludicrous claims about me and my character angers me to no end, let alone his repeated threats against me and my family.

ME: He's made direct threats?

MR. EGHBALI: Yes! I only hope this interview convinces the authorities to act faster, because, as I said, we're terrified. That's all I will say about that matter for now. Just wanted to set the record straight. I don't want to give that nonsense more attention than it's already gotten.

ME: That's understandable. Thank you for your time, Mr. Eghbali.

The OC Register reached out to Mr. Abbas Ebrahimi for a statement. He wrote the following:

> *"The truth about Mr. Eghbali and his corrupt business will come out eventually. When that day comes, he must answer to the Iranian people."*

***

February 6th, 2023

Abbas Ebrahimi posted:

I just read the OC Register's latest puff piece about Mullah Eghbali. Talk about dropping the ball! I don't know much about this so-called "journalist" Dalia Ashouri, but I suspect that she also has some ties to the Islamic Republic given that she follows PAAC on social media and hasn't shared that many posts about protests in Iran or Mahsa Amini since September. Rather unusual for an Iranian American millennial woman who calls herself a "feminist" hmmmmm....

But anway, even with her softball questions, I don't see how anyone can read that mans statements and not see right through his blatant lies. By the way the reason they never granted him a restraining order against me was that nothing about the emails I sent him and his family were threats. I only reminded them of the crimes in Iran that they are complicit in. Never the less I'm sick and tired of the inaction of the FBI in putting an end to what is obviously a MONEY LAUNDERING OPERATION here on American soil. Of course, under President Brandon, rest assured that our government will do nothing to stop the Islamic Republic and its agents here in America. In fact, they will CONTINUE sending them BILLIONS while they murder and rape Iranians in the streets! There is now also no doubt in my mind that the same George Soros-funded globalist scums who own CNN, NBC, BBC, etc. are also running the OC Register because that pathetic "article" reeks of their usual smokescreens and lies. But THE TRUTH WILL COME OUT. Believe me, the truth will comes out eventually.

WOMAN, LIFE, FREEDOM!

***

SUPERIOR COURT OF CALIFORNIA, County of ORANGE

Marriage of:
PETITIONER: Sara Ebrahimi
RESPONDENT: Abbas Ebrahimi

Petition for:
Dissolution of Marriage

DATE OF MARRIAGE: 10/07/1994
DATE OF SEPARATION: 02/24/2023
TIME FROM DATE OF MARRIAGE TO DATE OF SEPARATION:
28 years, 4 months

***

Daddy this is the last time I'm texting you before I file a missing persons report. Please come home

***

March 20th, 2023

Abbas Ebrahimi posted:

Collusion with the Islamic Republic goes deeper than any of us can imagine. Trump tried to warn us about the mullah-friendly Deep State and right now their punishing him for it. The blood of Mahsa is on their hands! They've brainwashed all those close to you and make US look like the crazy ones. Tomorrow they will call me crazy. They will call me a conspiracy theorist. They will call me a terrorist. But my heart is with the PEOPLE OF IRAN! My heart is with my dear parents, who died wishing they could one day finally return to their beloved home. My heart is with DEMOCRACY AND FREEDOM FOR IRAN! If my actions bring us just one step closer to that, than I have succeeded.

WOMAN, LIFE, FREEDOM!

***

THE ORANGE COUNTY REGISTER
3/21/2023

Local Man Sets Himself on Fire in Wholesome Ranch Market

Abbas Ebrahimi, a 62-year-old engineer living in Laguna Niguel, walked into Wholesome Ranch Market yesterday morning carrying a container of gasoline. Witnesses reported that he remained silent as he poured the gasoline onto himself and used a lighter to set himself on fire. Footage captured by the store's security cameras shows customers scrambling to put out the fire. Ebrahimi was alive but in critical condition when he was taken to Providence Mission Hospital in Mission Viejo, where he is currently being treated for severe burns.

Ebrahimi had previously made statements alleging that the store's owner Ali Eghbali was an agent of the Islamic Republic of Iran, and that Wholesome Ranch Market was part of a money laundering operation. In an interview with the OC Register last month, Eghbali denied the allegations. Ebrahimi was even present at and alleged to have incited a small protest in front of the store in January.

Those close to Ebrahimi describe him as a "loving family man" and "proud Iranian-American" whose behavior seemed to have taken a downward spiral since September of 2022. In that month, the death of his mother coincided with the alleged murder of 22-year-old Mahsa Amini at the hands of Iran's morality police.

"He'd always been outspoken about his opinions when it came to Iran," an anonymous family member says. *"But Mahsa's death and the protests that came afterwards, that was the last straw for him. He believed it was the responsibility of Iranians in America to be the voice of the protesters and join them in their calls for regime change."*

Ebrahimi, who emigrated from Iran in 1981, is married with a son and a daughter who are both in their twenties. His wife recently filed for divorce. They have all declined to comment and have chosen to remain anonymous, requesting privacy from the media.

Ali Eghbali has also denied our request for a statement.

ACKNOWLEDGEMENTS

As it turns out, moving from screenwriting to prose-writing is difficult. I thank Mercedes Garcia for her support (creative and emotional) from all the way back when *The Island of Stability* began life as a screenplay. On that note, I'd be remiss if I didn't thank Michael Weller, Aaron Covaleski, and Monna Sabouri—whose feedback on the screenplay version, in one way or another, convinced me that this would be the perfect medium for that story. I'd also like to thank Jessica Svelander for her meticulous editing and proofreading of my mess of a manuscript. Lastly, I express my deepest gratitude to my parents, who—as much as we bicker over our differing political views—raised me to be the politically and socially conscious person I am today.

The majority of the historical documents featured in the novella were easily accessible thanks to the tireless research efforts of the Mossadegh Project. Other resources that were invaluable to my research process were *The Last Shah* by Ray Takeyh, *The Fall of Heaven* by Andrew Scott Cooper, *The Shah* by Abbas Milani, *Answer to History* and *The Shah's Story* by Mohammad Reza Pahlavi, and *Winds of Change* by Reza Pahlavi.

I dedicate this book to all those who have been and continue to be displaced and oppressed as a consequence of imperialism.

ABOUT THE AUTHOR

Omid Iranikhah (oh-MEED ee-RAH-nekuh) is a filmmaker and now, an author. He has been a recipient of the Michael Collyer Memorial Fellowship in Screenwriting for his Iran-set folk horror screenplay *The Stoning of a Temptress*. Along with Mercedes Garcia, he co-founded the production company Stray Cats Productions, under which he has so far directed the award-winning short films *Don't Be a Stranger* and *Coffee With Baba*.